James Wills

An Estimate of the Antecedent Probablity of the Christian Religion

James Wills

An Estimate of the Antecedent Probablity of the Christian Religion

ISBN/EAN: 9783744744379

Printed in Europe, USA, Canada, Australia, Japan

Cover: Foto ©Lupo / pixelio.de

More available books at **www.hansebooks.com**

Works Published by the same Author.

LETTERS ON THE PHILOSOPHY OF UNBELIEF.

8vo. boards, price 7s.

LONDON: B. FELLOWES.

VESTIGES OF GOD IN SCRIPTURE,

IN TWO ACT SERMONS,

PREACHED IN

THE CHAPEL OF TRINITY COLLEGE, DUBLIN,

MAY 20th, 1855, and JUNE 22nd, 1856.

8vo. sewed, price 1s.

DUBLIN: HODGES, SMITH, & CO. 104, GRAFTON-STREET,
Booksellers to the University.

AN ESTIMATE

OF THE

ANTECEDENT PROBABILITY

OF THE

CHRISTIAN RELIGION,

AND OF ITS MAIN DOCTRINES,

IN

SIX SERMONS

PREACHED IN THE CHAPEL OF TRINITY COLLEGE, DUBLIN;

Being the Donnellan Lectures for 1858.

BY

JAMES WILLS, D.D. M.R.I.A.

AUTHOR OF LETTERS ON THE PHILOSOPHY OF UNBELIEF.

Τὰ γὰρ ἀόρατα αὐτοῦ ἀπὸ κτίσεως κόσμου τοῖς ποιήμασι νοούμενα καθορᾶται.

DUBLIN:
HODGES, SMITH, AND CO. 104, GRAFTON STREET,
Booksellers to the University.

1860.

PRINTED BY R. D. WEBB, GREAT BRUNSWICK-STREET.

THESE DISCOURSES

ARE INSCRIBED TO

THE RIGHT REVEREND

THE LORD BISHOP OF OSSORY, LEIGHLIN AND FERNS,

WITH PROFOUND RESPECT

FOR HIS EMINENT STATION AND CHARACTER AS A SCHOLAR, DIVINE,

AND FAITHFUL OVERSEER AND SENTINEL

OF THE CHURCH MILITANT OF CHRIST ON EARTH,

BY HIS FAITHFUL AND AFFECTIONATE SERVANT,

THE AUTHOR.

PREFACE.

In the way of preface I have little to say. The title of this volume is perhaps in some degree likely to deter those for whose benefit it is mainly designed; as it may seem to promise a highly speculative discussion and a metaphysical style of language—now become prevalent among the antagonists of modern sceptical philosophy. This has been forced upon many able divines who have undertaken to contend with the rationalism of a foreign school: but, however useful it may be in the counteraction of an infidel philosophy, it has introduced a tone of discussion far above the intellect of the educated multitude. I think it for this reason not wholly needless to explain at the outset, the actual character and design of the method of the following Discourses. Whatever degree of originality I may claim for the argument in its general application, the matter of its premises is scrupulously selected from the most familiar topics of popular intelligence, or the most established facts of social life. Nor have I been less careful, at whatever cost of scientific or logical precision, to preserve the most intelligible language in colloquial use.

As my argument ultimately rests upon those laws of probability which are the laws of common sense, and to reasonable minds require no proof, it was necessary to clear away some fallacies which affect these, the very foundations of all reason. This portion of my task I have wholly transferred to an introduction, not absolutely essential to the following discourses, nor to be recommended to any reader whose intellect is undisturbed by the insubstantial logic of terms, called rationalism. In the very limited notice of such fallacies as I have found it expedient to discuss, I have endeavoured to bring them within the verge of intelligible sense, by reverting to their earlier and abler expositors, and by translating them into the ordinary language of the world.

CONTENTS.

INTRODUCTION.

                                                                                PAGE.

Design of the argument—Principle of reason—Opposed by sceptical theories—These injudiciously met by modern theists—Practically stated and answered—Idealism and causality—False view of laws of nature—Method proposed . . .   1

FIRST LECTURE.

Genesis, i. 26.

First principle stated—Applied to the existence of a Creator—Purpose—Indicated by adaptation—This illustrated—Man the main design—Purpose of man's creation—This resolved into two theories, a final present, or a final future . . .   21

SECOND LECTURE.

Psalm, xc. 3.

Conditions of inquiry, and limitations on either assumption—Elements of social theory fully known—Interruptions and retardations not admissible—Nature of man inconsistent with this theory—Its rejection   39

THIRD LECTURE.

Psalm, cxix. 96.

heory of a final future—Conditions of the question—Man's necessity of original instruction—A religious knowledge inferred—Such traceable to earliest records—Argued from human superstitions—One religion only indicates the requisite claims—Should be a revelation—Authenticated—Continuous through time—Adapted to the state of man, present and future, by certain moral and doctrinal adaptations   63

SECOND PART.

FOURTH LECTURE.

Romans, iii. 23.

State of man examined—Proved abnormal—Generally—Individually—Remedial provisions necessary—Doctrinal provisions—Spiritual aid—Vicarious satisfaction   91

FIFTH LECTURE.

1 Corinthians, xiii. 13.

Moral standard—Faith, hope, charity—Peculiarity of the combination—Faith a main principle of action—Special adaptations—Charity in relation to life—To a future state   113

SIXTH LECTURE.

Galatians, iii. 21.

Antecedent objection to doctrines—Speculative theology—Imperfect comprehension of the Divine scheme a true answer, but not satisfactory—Conditional method explained—Answers the sceptic on his own grounds—Conclusive so far as regards the objection—First case selected, the Atonement—Second, the existence of evil   137

NOTES.

NOTE A.—Language, Letters, Civilisation 173
NOTE B.—The Jews 182
NOTE C.—The soul 189
NOTE D.—Evidences 202
NOTE E.—Temptation 211
NOTE F.—The universe 213

INTRODUCTION.

There is in most minds, more or less, a latent incredulity, variously operative, respecting the unseen, unknown, and inconceivable, however capable of proof. This condition of mind is nearly universal. And there often exists, concurrently with the assent of reason, a want of that habitual conviction on which men act in the ordinary courses of life. I have, in a small volume published many years ago, endeavoured to explain and trace to their ordinary results the various workings consequent upon this fundamental infirmity.* How it leads to

---

* "Letters on the Philosophy of Unbelief." Fellowes: London, 1835. The distinction between faith and mere intellectual assent, or mere belief, perhaps may require more explanation than I am here enabled to afford. I should, however, say more but that I am happily enabled to avail myself of a higher authority than any work of mine. The following extract is from the well-known "Sermons on Justification," by Dr. O'Brien (since, Bishop of Ossory), and fully expresses the condition, to which I would advert. " Investigating the subject on sounder principles, in a more patient course, and in a humble spirit, you, my brethren, will find, I am persuaded, that the true nature of Faith, when we are most concerned to ascertain its meaning, is TRUST. That the true meaning, therefore, *of faith in Christ, or in God through Christ*, is not merely, or properly, belief in the scripture narrative concerning our Lord ; or an assent of the understanding to certain propositions derived

neglect and remissness in the professing Christian; or, in the questioning and incredulous, to confirmed scepticism.

This common tendency may be otherwise described as an impression of antecedent improbability in all that cannot be reduced within the scope of habitual conception or sensible phenomena—the unimaginable and the unseen. It is easy to conceive the ordinary case of a person habitually negligent of religious concerns, unspiritual in temper and inclinations, and unacquainted with the rational grounds upon which Christianity is understood to stand. To such a person, if once any question should from any cause arise, the circumstantial and doctrinal facts of the New Testament will be likely to appear under the aspect of antecedent improbability. The constraining power of habitual observance being unfelt, spiritual influences wanting, and the evidences unknown—there can exist no bar against the sceptical tendencies of human nature. In this case there will often rise up the sense of inability to believe, so often and not untruly pleaded, and a consequent distrust in the possibility of any *satisfactory* proof: a reluctance to be perplexed to no end, and deluded into restraints of conscience by subtle reasoning, on matters antecedently improbable. Generally speaking, the arguments of the sceptic are as little known as the proofs of revealed religion, but, like

from that narrative, however true, and however important they be; but that it is TRUST IN CHRIST, OR IN GOD THROUGH CHRIST, founded on an such assent; an entire and unreserved confidence in what Christ has done and suffered for us: a full reliance on Him and on His work," p. 13. The bare assent of reason, without this confident trust, is the common condition I would describe.

them, are received on trust: it is pleaded that many great philosophers have rejected Christianity : with the writings of these famed persons few are acquainted and still fewer understand them ; but the effect is the same,— an added prejudice, on seeming grounds of reason.

It may be mentioned as an unhappy aggravation of these fallacious impressions, that the crowd of Christian believers entertain a very strange distrust of all rational inquiry. For the faithful Christian, on whom habit, experience, and grace have done their proper work, natural and spiritual, proof may be superfluous; but this prejudice becomes communicated to those who have not their advantages. The common cant has arisen, that Christian belief is exclusively the result of what is called implicit faith. Against this idle prejudice it might be replied, that every Christian who has intelligence to think on the subject is aware that the proof, if wanted, exists in the most undoubted and authentic records, in the clearest testimonies and repositories of history, in the reasonings of the most learned scholars of eighteen centuries, and in the total failure of all adverse attempts. The same universal acceptance through all the Christian periods—which is, to the world, the ground of all other persuasions—vouches for a faith which could never have stood against all sorts of trials which it has had to meet, one hundredth part of the time, unless sustained by inexpugnable evidence and divine power.

The object of the following discourses is to maintain the proposition, that so far from the existence of any antecedent improbability in the facts or doctrines of Christianity, there is, on the contrary, an antecedent probability of the highest order in their favor: such, indeed, that it cannot be obviated but by the abandonment of the first principles of reason. That this strange resource has for ages, but more especially in modern times, been among the aims of sceptical philosophy, will be scarcely denied. But for this I might here close these introductory remarks. But the nature and whole drift of the argument stated in the following lectures demand some preliminary notice of the subtleties which pretend to subvert the elementary principles on which its very first step must be fixed,—the essential basis of all probable reasoning.

Sceptical rationalism, coeval with human error, has from the time of Hume and Berkeley grown to a formidable stature and compass of influence. It has in a great measure abandoned the practicable defences of plain language and popular reason, and entrenched itself within the inaccessible depths of a profound and elaborate terminology, which, if it does not add to its strength, at least serves to conceal its weakness, and to baffle the ordinary approach of common sense. When a great and dangerous fallacy appears sustained by illustrious names, it is to be combated at considerable disadvantage; and this most especially when the task is to be executed within the brief limit which my present object will allow. I cannot, consistently with my purpose, launch out into the ocean of obscure terminology, which conceals so much expert logic and so many refined oppositions. The rationalist will, after all, be only approachable in his first assumption. A wholly unwarrantable assertion is invested in terms which are managed with all the precision of algebraic symbols, and the systematic precision of the subsequent process appears to confirm inferences, which (if they have a distinct meaning) can have no more value than the false or doubtful assumption on which they rest. A contest with such methods is out of the question. Fortunately, I am only concerned with this class of questions so far as they may seem to affect the fundamental assumption of the following inquiry.

There are two very obvious methods (so far as we are here concerned) of reviewing the sceptical theory. We may follow the varied lines of verbal reasoning to the inferences as various, to which they appear to lead, or seek the direct disproof by establishing the contrary conclusions. For brevity and simplicity, and, indeed, as the only intelligible course, I shall be content to adopt the latter method. Many have, I must be allowed to say injudiciously, taken the first method, and only aggravated the perplexity of such inquiries by the adoption of the same vague method, or by the concessions into which they have been inadvertently led, or by the doubts which they have stumbled over in the tortuous maze of subtle fallacies. At the same time it is impossible to avoid the concession, that the course I now propose is open to the heavy disadvantage of appearing to prove what nobody but a philosopher, far gone from the world of sense, can doubt. If we attempt to convince any person of ordinary intelligence that the sun shines, or that he walks on firm ground, no jest in Punch or Joe Miller would be surer to elicit a laugh. But these philosophical inferences, not very far remote from the same description, present themselves in the disguise of vague theories and cloaked by subtle questions, consequences, and foregone conclusions, and by the *prestige* of illustrious names.

The theories to which I shall now have to ask the reader's patient attention for a few pages, are only important as being immediately opposed to the first principle of the subsequent statements; I am, therefore, compelled to a brief notice, at the cost of offending against the high theoretic dignity of the philosopher, or the common sense which may be outraged by the proof of truisms. I may well be told that no proof can be required to confirm the evidence of every sense, and we are sure that (practically) no sceptic believes his own theories.

It, however so happens, that when, as in the proposed inquiry, it becomes necessary to ascend to the first principles of probable reasoning, the first propositions with which we have to deal, stand upon the very basis against which the sceptical philosophy has directed its whole force. And however worthless its reasonings or glaringly absurd its conclusions, still a vague and lurking suspicion is thrown upon the very language essential to reason. This must be my apology for a few statements, which, to many, must seem wholly uncalled for.

Both the ideal and causal theories, however varied, rest ultimately on a common fallacy. It is alleged that, as the immediate relation or elementary *nexus* between either mind and matter, or between effect and cause, cannot be discerned or sensibly traced, they may, therefore, be assumed to have no existence, or (as some more moderate will have it) at furthest, cannot be *assumed* to exist. If admitted to have any value, it seems plain that of such conclusions universal scepticism is the result; if carried to their legitimate conclusion, the whole creation is resolved into the idea of the sceptic's brain; nor has reason a spot of solid ground on which to stand.

It is quite true that *one* completely isolated mind, fixed to a point of space, and not reasoning too closely on phenomena, might easily imagine itself and all the surrounding spectacle to be a dream. If this were all, the illusion could not well be dispelled by reason, of which the main instruments are experimental and comparative. We cannot confute Hume or Berkeley by asserting *as known* the elementary facts they deny. All we can do in this respect is to tell them that the whole use and force of experience go against their theory.

But it is fairly open to us to demonstrate the fact which we cannot see or sensibly apprehend. The laws of occurrence (as I shall presently show) by no means rest on the evidence of mere observation, but are subject to that of number and mathematical computation, and are throughout ascertainable in their laws and results, prior to experience or the evidences of sense. The computation which fixes the existence of an unseen planet, or discovers conical refraction antecedent to the experimental proof, amounts, in actual value, to the demonstration of a law, and meets the double requisition both of the external fact and causal relation. But before I enter on this truth, I have to add two general observations. When the supposed idealist, leaving his philosophical isolation, moves abroad into life, communicates, changes place, handles and sees in varied aspects of reality, he must, if not wholly enslaved by abstractions, soon apprehend many distinctions between the dream and the reality. As I suppose him to be a philosopher, and to have studied the laws of mind, he may be astonished to discover that, while morally and intellectually he has within his consciousness a complete and highly complex system of reason, passion, and sentiment, he is dreaming, or is affected by the appearance of another far wider and more complex system of laws of occurrence, beyond all influences of his will, and even of his understanding. In addition to this—a seemingly external system, comprising other beings like himself, governed by complicated systems of law and policy, to which he finds himself subject, yet does not wholly comprehend; for the legal sage has no such dreams. Now so far may be illustrated the common ground for the faith of mankind, to which it will be enough to add, that a law of the mind compels this belief: a strong *prima facie* ground for the testimony of sense. This enormous complication of systems thus describable, moral, intellectual, and visionary with the apprehension of a still larger external system, is in itself wholly irreconcilable with the simplicity and order otherwise perceptible throughout all the realm of observation.* It has neither speciousness nor antecedent probability, and rests but on a theory of evasions and overstrained possibilities. It is more reasonable (were other evidence wanting) to assume the truth of the perceptions of sense, than to ad-

---

* It was, perhaps, this difficulty which constrained Berkeley to refer the perceptions and ideas of an external world to an immediate source in the divine mind—surely the most extravagant notion in the list of philosophical chimeras, and leading to inferences most irreconcilable with Berkeley's theology.

mit without proof, on the force of negative premises, so vast and irreconcilable a complication.

The extreme futility of the ideal theory may be shewn from the instances which Mr. Hume has used for its support. This eminent sophist exemplifies the unreality of external objects, from the variations in form and dimension which seem to meet the sense at different distances and positions. Now, it is too plain for explanation or proof, that were this variation wanting, it would be the sure proof of the unreality of the object, as the apparent change is the necessary and calculable result of the change of distance or position, insomuch that the mutual relations of distance and apparent diameter of a given magnitude are subjects of the nicest accuracy of mathematical computation. The firmest theory would sink under the weight and complexity of such facts.

But the case is stronger still. The ideal sceptic must assume himself to be the only mind in existence. He can offer for the contrary assumption no reason that must not abandon his theory. If such be his conclusion, we may leave him "alone in his glory." If he admits other persons to be real, and what they seem, he must then be aware of the fact that others, having the same senses and scope of observation, shew by act, word, writing, and calculation that they have a common compass of observation. Now a table, a chair, or a house, *seen by one*, may be a dream, but to be simultaneously seen by many, it must be something external to all. Let two persons make a drawing of the object in different aspects and distances, and it will be represented according to the distance and aspect, in precise conformity to the laws of perspective, and the perception of the sense. I select this fallacy, not only because it leads to the true experimental treatment of idealism, but because it also very clearly illustrates the secret of philosophical rationalism in all its phases— *a tendency to strip every question of all its conditions*: the abstraction becomes thus subject to no test, and experience becomes an empty phrase, as abstract as the proposition to which it is applied. Hence the property noticed by Mr. Hume of the sceptical philosophy—to carry no conviction, yet admit no reply. The reply is, want of meaning: a want concealed in later times by an obscure and elaborate terminology. A language is to be learned, in order to descend into the mysteries of Kant and his illustrious fraternity.

The ideal theory was applied by Mr. Hume, to introduce his theory of causation ; and plainly destroys the assumption of cause. The same argument by which the former inference was obtained, was also, with some distrust of his previous reasoning, employed to establish the latter. The elementary operation which connects cause and effect cannot be ascertained with scientific certainty, and having affirmed this undeniable proposition, Mr. Hume assumed that no such relation had existence. Other, more modern essayists, doubtless dissatisfied with this summary, and, too obviously, inconclusive method, have invented various elaborate methods of arriving at similar results, and more sound thinkers in examining these fallacies, have in some instances been content with the simple affirmation of truth, or in others, entangled themselves in the fallacies so far as to concede too much for the cause of truth.

The direct method, which it is here proposed to follow, will render it needless to entangle the reader in these nugatory discussions, in which much valuable intellect has been sunk. The attempt, equally absurd and rash, to look for the primary elements and initial workings of either mind or matter, transgresses alike the limits of either sense, experience, or reason. The essential nature of substance, of the attractions and affinities by which forms and qualities are determined, and all the forces moral or physical throughout nature, are beyond the grasp of observation or certain inference. A line is to be determined, at which experimental science may begin within the scope of observation. And the question then becomes not, " why," but " how," the law of phenomena operates. A law of nature is not a constant sequence but a constant relation between phenomena, in force, measure, or intensity,—or a constant variation, wherein one so changes with the changes of the other, as to imply some regulating connexion. Such is the great law of reason, on which in some form every question of probability depends. It is ascertained by uniform experience, confirmed by all science and experiment,—impressed intuitively on every mind by countless results obedient to the will. There are few, if any, effects, or physical processes on earth, that cannot be produced by putting into action those agents which are known as causal. With the *mode of operation* reason is unconcerned, and can only be employed to lead inquiry astray, and cast the subject into mystification. Such, if the existence of the external world be admitted, are facts which leave no room for question, on which all science is founded, and to which all science bears testimony.

And what, in the mean time, is the criterion of causation? Is it that artfully proposed by Mr. Hume and his followers, with a view to nullify this relation—constant sequence? Assuredly not. It may be called a constant relation of proportion, a *co-ordinate variation*, by which more follows more, and less, less. When any two phenomena appear together, or in immediate succession, so that one varies with the intensity or direction of the other in any constant ratio, the presumption arises, that the one results from some efficacy of the other, or is in some way contained in it. This presumption is confirmed or modified by repeated observation or trial, and the principle will be no way weakened·by the analysis which in some cases may reduce an apparent cause to some prior element which it may involve.

If, in any case, there is room for doubt, it must be remembered that the principle has not been affirmed on the force of such cases, but upon the common evidence of the manifold experience, of which every act in life and all practical results in nature are instances,—every end of every purpose of man—every motion of the human frame—every force or material influence put in action for any end—every application of motives to persuade or compel, are all indications of the apprehension and proofs of the reality of causation. Numberless effects are connected with causes by weight and quantity; and the subtle and operose calculation which fixes a precise fact, thus confirmed by observation, at the same time offers the strongest proof of the causal relation between the fact seen and the fact so found. The whole science of political economy is a minute and complex reasoning on presumptions, involving the certainty of effects from causes. Effects or causes are operative conditions, both moral and physical, some of them liable to much uncertainty, from the multitude of their interferences and the various degrees of their combinations, concurrences, and oppositions; while the conclusiveness of reasoning is still understood to depend upon the constant and uniform operation among these elements; and the degree of uncertainty, upon the liability to error common to human reason in questions so wide, complex, and containing conditions so often latent. And this may answer for the description of the greater portion of human reasonings. All moral inferences on conduct proceed on the causal uniformity and subordination of motives, under, or free from the government of reason: these may offer a fair illustration of the complexity of the subject, in their combinations, contrarieties, and latent phases. Causes which are less affected by such conditions are inferred and measured with more uniform certainty. Gradations of effect in heat or light may be computed with numerical accuracy: similarly, the effects of gravitation have been traced to their common, though mysterious, cause, under appearances so different as to have baffled the philosophy of ages. The fall of a stone to the earth has been proved identical, as an effect, with the curvilinear motion of the moon in its orbit. Ten thousand measurable effects, mechanical or chemical, can be put into measured action at the will of man. On the uniform and co-ordinate variation of forces and results, of means and ends, applications and uses, motives and conduct, all reasoning that has reality for its object, depends. To look for the efficient principle of causation is but a lamentable waste of reason, only leading to some fallacy; and so far as it has been employed to any purpose, the result has been a denial of the very principle on which all reasoning (not simply proceeding from arbitrary definition) depends. An elementary treatise on the law of probable reasoning—not being merely arithmetical, or merely syllogistic—should consist of an estimate of probable effects from known causes, or probable causes from observed effects. Volumes on the subject could not make it clearer. The subject has been involved in endless obscurity, from the rejection of the one clear and simple aspect in which it offers itself to the human understanding; and a confusion of thought has been raised, which is in some measure concealed by a science of language in which there is no concord or fixed meaning. The true science of probable reasoning, applicable whenever reason can have any real application, has for its object the *law of occurrence*. In abstract science the inference is just, because it follows legitimately from the assumption, and depends on no concrete reality: rationalism assumes a proposition of which the terms have no true sense, and the conclusion is no truer than the premises.

But rationalism has an opposite phase, more dangerous, because more intelligible.

Of the known abuses of reason, materialism exceeds all, in its plain and, apparently, wilful absurdity. The idealist wanders far into the void of abstraction, and wastes his acute dialectic on empty words; the materialist moves purblind in the tracks of observation and experience, and while his near-sighted gaze fixes on some atomic particle or motion, he fails to apprehend the world of vast and complex phenomena to which it belongs. Pretending to observation, he fails to observe; and in ascribing to causation an underived supremacy, he excludes the universal range of phenomena that cannot be explained by his narrow scheme; by a theory which (in some cases), beginning in reality, is stretched beyond it at the second step; and, finding often imaginary grounds in his own mistakes, rivals the ideal philosopher in his departures from reality.

It is quite admissible, that supposing the philosophizing observer to set out from the point of a comprehensive ignorance, the investigation of some single process of nature, and wholly unaware of any other, he might excusably imagine its law of development to be an original, self-existent law—because, until something to the contrary appears, one uncompounded principle of being may as well be assumed to have always existed as another. Had we nothing to explain but the known simple effect of gravitation, it would be hard to answer the materialist who might take this for his universal solution. Had we nothing but some simple form of animal existence, we should have little certain objection to the theory of development, some years since proposed by Mr. Lawrence and others of his school, but its want of of proof, and amusing absurdity. Suppose nothing but the sun and planets to have existence, or some vegetable, or even some one animal organization (if this conception were simplified into possibility); and taking separately *any one* such instance, as containing the *whole problem of being*, the inference would not be logically inadmissible, that it may possibly be a result of such processes as might best explain its origination ; or, to vary our illustration, if some profound philosoper, fresh from the moon, were to meet here below some one work of art, he might in this first instance not unreasonably refer to it some process of physical development. Presently, however, he would discover its connexion with a large system of dissimilar things, wholly independent in composition and structure, but all forming together essential parts of a broad system of contrivance indicating a common purpose, and connected by one bond of subserviency to human use. Such then is the originating law to which he should be conducted in the result. Thus the philosopher, who takes the solar system apart from the sum of things ; or human, or vegetable physiology ; in each instance shutting his understanding against all beside ; may easily concoct a lucid and ingenious theory like that of M. La Place,[*] or with Surgeon Lawrence derive man from some aboriginal oyster.

But one true and clear-eyed glance upon the broad scene of varied life in nature inexhaustible in form and mode of existence of distinct and independent natures, all working together without confusion, must be enough to scatter into dust these idols of the school.

I have no objection to admit the elementary exposition of many varied processes of structural development ; they only want reasonable proof, and are mostly empirical.

---

[*] Systeme du Monde, liv. v. c. 6.

The question here is not as to their possibility or impossibility. The materialist's error lies in the intent and the inference ; separately taken, his premises may, by a remote possibility, be true; but the inference is *manifestly* false, that he thus has excluded the necessity of some higher combining principle of the whole. The material principle, taken so far as it has any true application, goes no farther than this, that the creative Power uses means to ends ; that he has created forces, attractions, and affinities, with subtle elements of production and formative efficacy, too refined for the grossness of human sense. If, by some incredible reach of sense and intellect, these and such elements should be so known as to explain the development of man, or that of horse, or tree, or corn, or light, or heat, still the chain of use, order, mutual operation, and adaptation by which these are connected into one system, has to be found. For this the materialist must be entirely at fault ; what he pretends to explain is trifling, to what he leaves unexplained. It is not sun, or planet, or earth, or man, or herb, but all their phenomena and all their uses together—woods, and waters, and vegetation, and varied life, and varied provisions for the sustenance of all: so that the material object is far less than the immaterial principle of universal adaptation, the manifestation of purpose and contrivance, a principle external to all, as is the time of day to the wheels and springs of a watch ; or, to revert to natural phenomena, as the adjustment of the earth's axis, separate from, yet essential for the rotation of crops and their seasons, in neither of which can the common principle be found, until sought in some previous adapting power, independent of all. So the ear is independent of sound, the eye of light, the whole digestive apparatus of food. Now, if the theorist faithfully follows out his chain of causal deduction sufficiently far to conduct him to this external element, and fairly attempts to infer its nature and description from its manifest uses and operations, he must find himself fairly and inevitably landed in definitions of mind and its known operations. Neither, if the whole of the varied display of nature be contemplated, will any attribute of mind be wanting. To this ultimate resource the atheist is often inadvertently driven, when he feels compelled to *personify nature*, and ascribe to it all the faculties which he denies to God. He might often be addressed in the words of Paul to the Athenians, " Whom ye ignorantly worship, Him declare I unto you."

The materialist has not only to explain the fact of the existence of mind, but he has to meet the difficulty of its indications, which are involved in all things. His error does not consist in the assumption of causative laws, but in not recognizing the necessity as well as the indications of a higher law from a higher and more comprehensive source, combining, reconciling, and governing all—a source of intent, design, method, and purpose; in a word, the same principle in an infinitely wider and higher form, of which he has experimental acquaintance in himself and his fellow-creatures; with just the difference, that in the latter it is erring, feeble, and confined within a narrow sphere of thought and action ; in the former, unerring, all-pervading, and all-ruling, supreme over all powers, and the origin of all.

It is curious to remark the art of evasion and verbal

ambiguity by which the broadest imaginable absurdities can be smoothed away into the semblance of some not irrational meaning. A German rationalist of no small authority, of whose theory I have just been engaged in the perusal, has managed to give a religious tone to his book by frequent respectful allusions to the Supreme Being; but, on close inspection, his god melts away into public opinion and sentiment. With this new species of positivism it would be childish to argue, until its aim and effect shall become more perceptible. In all forms of rationalism—while it is to be admitted that they indicate much ingenuity, and, in some instances, dialectic skill—there is a want of intellectual sobriety and soundness common to all.

In the infidel communities which prevail in some parts of Europe, it is easy to understand the latitude of opinion by which such theories will pass without question, and the ambition by which they will be elaborated. But in Christian England they can have little comparative effect, and will mostly be found connected with youthful inexperience, levity, or eccentricity. Extreme activity of mind is often to be met, with remarkable inconsequence of judgment; the youthful mind, having yielded to the charm of extreme subtlety, and of a verbal science far above vulgar apprehension, easily dismisses reality from its sphere of apprehension; and, becoming involved in the fascination of an imaginary science, the adoption of the sceptical theory soon reconciles the mind to refinements which lead to nothing—truth ceases to be an object of aim or belief, and the subtleties of a ponderous system of aimless logic become all in all to the infatuated student.

* Hegel.

But, finally, if they were to be allowed the most extreme conclusions of sceptical theories, if the world and the whole phenomena of mind and matter were to be set down as unreal, it is to be observed that there exists no ground for the exclusion of the practical concerns of life. If these are admitted by the youthful rationalist to have the value which his whole conduct proves him to admit, it may be suggested that all he would deny stands on the same ground of certainty. The rules of reason for all that he admits, apply to all that he denies, and there are no others practically applicable. If his being is a dream, he is wholly shut in within that dream ; and while he practically admits one fact, he cannot in reason deny the other ; all that he recognizes as true ; the rules of reason applicable to all he knows, or sees, or acts, prove all his theories to be chimerical.

The many topics which have offered matter of argument or illustration, in the course of these lectures, have seemed, for the same reasons, to claim much further extension. I might also have derived much valuable confirmation from many authors, had the limited extent of this work, and the stipend allotted by the worthy founder of the lecture, permitted. I am, however, under the impression that so far as the validity of my inferences requires, no essential addition is wanting. The need for which I have written is in a manner popular ; and it will, I trust, be seen, that I have carefully avoided the recondite phraseology with which many able writers have, of late, fenced their theological and metaphysical theories.

LECTURE I.

Gen. i. 26.—"Let us make man in our own image, after our likeness: and let them have dominion over the fish of the sea, and over the fowl of the air, and over the cattle, and over all the earth."

The first proposition on which the course of inquiry which I have undertaken to pursue, must mainly depend, rests upon the same elementary principle which is the foundation of all probable reasoning, and from which it will be found to follow as a direct inference, inevitable without some departure from the law of reason. The universal first principle of causation, which pervades all known existence with a uniformity which admits of no exception, and a certainty that admits of no rational disproof, and the broad analogy which is its practical inference, have been already explained.* The application here designed is one of extreme simplicity. For my present purpose the theory of causes may be stated thus —that similar effects must be referred to similar causes.

---

* Introduction. As these arguments were first delivered in a form which excluded the convenience of a prefatory statement, it may be necessary to mention that this explanation was included in the above discourse, but in a form too compressed for the importance of the place it held, in the first step of a popular inquiry. To give it due expansion, and also to preserve the utmost attainable simplicity, I have thought proper to transfer it to the separate medium of a preface.

The case excludes the necessity of any exceptional reserve.

When we trace to its proximate origin any complex combination of means to an end, in any instance which offers full means for such a scrutiny—that is, *in any human contrivance*—we shall uniformly find the search terminate in one manifest element. Wherever there is to be discerned a systematic co-operation of mutually independent means, in which the origin *can be* traced that origin is, in every instance, *mind*—the sole known, or even conceivable originating element in any case, bearing the character of contrivance. Such is a fact of universal experience; and it follows from the fundamental law of reason, that in like cases of combination, of which the origin *is not to be so traced*, the like effect must be still referred to the like cause unknown; the working together of independent instrumentalities and systems of instrumentality, to effect a discernible end, must in reason be similarly understood, and as the complication becomes broader and more various, and the end more observable, this conclusion obtains greater force. The observed operations are not only to be ascribed to the ascertained originating element of mind, but in a great measure will appear to represent its essential attributes. Such, within the limit of observation, is the system of the world—a system of countless, separate, and independent contrivances, co-operating to produce one harmonious whole. Of such a system it is not only to be inferred, with Cicero, Paley, and other authorities, that it cannot be a result of chance, or any accidental juxta-position of elements, but that it must be in all its parts an effect from those faculties and powers of which the operations appear in the phenomenal results. The world is not merely a system, but a system of innumerable systems, each having its own law or working process, while the whole, in which all are integrally combined, is unaffected by the law of operation discernible in any of its parts. A thousand living and moving processes, each wholly different in its nature and proximate source, meet in a point of being, to indicate an intent and controlling power, itself distinct from all. The train is not more pre-arranged for its iron road, the sail for the wind, or the ship for the sea, than the eye, framed from its earthly material and process, for the light propagated from its source one hundred million miles away. Such are the relations throughout nature—the sound and the ear, the cattle and the pasture " on a thousand hills," the bee and the flower, the air and the wing. No volume could contain the list of indications solely resolvable into *purpose;* plain proofs of supreme, all-controlling faculties—will, plan, purpose, knowledge, adaptation,—an intelligence infinitely wider than the bounded intellect to which I have compared its workings. If we were to conceive a volume of natural history comprizing a full analysis of all known natures, with their combinations and uses, including animal habits and propensities, such a volume should also offer the most accurate exemplification of every *operation of reason*, or, what is here more strictly applicable, every *result* of mental powers and attributes; all that reason, all that conception, all that contrivance and constructive skill can effectuate. It is no objection to say, that of the depth and complex combination, as well as of the boundless compass of these realities in nature, all that man can learn would fall infinitely short: but would such an exposition be thought accountable otherwise than by presuming the application of every higher operation of mental power, or could the examples so offered bear any explanation short of the same attributes which they should thus seem to represent? The working together of the varied multitude of mutual independencies, among which relations tending to results; all stamped with the autograph of a predetermining Reason, are so combined, not in words and sentences, but in a compact and immeasurable system of realities—the million trains of realized premises which are combined into one first conclusion proportionably vast, not in human writing, but stereotyped on infinite space by the eternal mind.

The phenomena of the natural world not only indicate the attributes of a mind of proportioned power, but, as you must have already observed, the preceding statements essentially imply two other inseparable conditions—a purpose, and a law of adaptation, its necessary instrument. Purpose is necessarily implied in the definition of design, contrivance, or invention, by whatever term they may be implied: in all, purpose is a plain antecedent; and the operative means by which a purpose can be effected are, properly, *adaptations*. From these adaptations, as also from such actual ends as the observation of nature can supply, we may legitimately seek to ascertain what may have been the immediate purpose of the Contriver. This inquiry is subject to another condition, by reason of the narrowness of human knowledge, only applicable with great caution and within narrow limits: that purpose must bear some proportion to the power and intellectual compass of the Being to whom it is to be ascribed. In the boundless field of creation we cannot hope to trace out ends which may be far hidden in the depths of the eternal counsel; and, therefore, no adverse inference can generally follow from the absence *(if not exclusive,)* of definite indications; while we may justly conclude from those which we can clearly substantiate as systematically pervading any department of nature; and, above all, it is to be kept in view, that such ends as appear clearly provided for by means ascribable to the supreme Contriver, must be taken to be among his purposed ends. All these conditions will be very fully illustrated in the application, to which I shall immediately come.

But as the first and most important propositions connected with this inquiry must consist chiefly in the application of the principle of *adaptation*, it may add to the clearness of this application to offer a very familiar example, which, to those not much accustomed to such considerations, will explain the argumentative value of this principle, and illustrate the compass and precision of the test it affords when applied to the works of a Power which " does nothing in vain."

Every educated person is now aware of the method employed by M. Cuvier, for the identification of the fossil remains of extinct animals with the probable structure and habits of the living creature. How a broken fragment—a slight curve of bone, a minute and fretted process enabled that sagacious observer to assign the order and habits of the animal in its integral form and living state. Many here will recollect the singular and wonderful confirmatory instance, which should have imparted a telling shock to the self-reliance of sceptical philosophy, when the gigantic animal which the philosophic anatomist had reasoned out from antecedent probability, and constructed on the evidence of refined adaptations, and which, to a mind of inferior sagacity, might have passed for a monster of fiction, was (in its bodily reality) disinterred from its primeval sepulchre of arctic snows. Our present examples of the same law, in the course of these lectures, will be far less adventurous.

Now, these considerations being understood, the first question which offers is this: what, in probability, is the main purpose of this province of creation which is the abode of the human race—our earthly world, with its aggregate of being?

According to the foregoing grounds of inference, and from other statements of fact on which no doubt rests, it will easily and clearly be inferred that the main apparent purpose of this province of creation is the existence and destiny of the human race.

Before looking into those detailed adaptations, which by the conditions of the argument are to be sought for, we meet at the outset a very striking fact, which seems of itself to decide the question. The actual mastery and main occupation of the earth and all it holds, is in the human race. Man holds possession of the planet—a result which cannot be assumed to be without the intent and direct cognizance of the designer and organizer of both. This argument will be strengthened by some views of man's own nature and history, which I shall hereafter briefly state. But the conditions of the previous statement require that we should first take a summary view of the obvious or ascertained adaptations for his occupation of the world, as described.

When we look for the provisions for man adopted by the Supreme Artificer, we are met by the clear evidence of a wonderful succession of arrangements, illustrative of the boundless Power to which duration and space can be of no account in the scale of operation—to whom " a thousand years are as a day." It stands ascertained upon grounds on which all warrantable doubt has long ceased, that for vast periods antecedent to the recorded epoch of man's creation, a succession of slow revolutions of the structure, constitution, and living occupancy of this planet, began to prepare the varied materials for the system of human life, and the dominion which man holds. And it should be observed by those who might be in any way startled by the conception of a course so seemingly protracted, that such has (to the full extent of observation and experience) been the uniform method of the divine economy, which, in all its operations, has ever seemed to approach remote ends by an ascending series of distinct steps of creation. Of this, man's own history is but an instance. But the inference in the present instance is grounded on the plain fact, that the successive results of those planetary changes, are the well known products which are the essential materials, without which the social state of man could not exist—the coals, the minerals, and the soils. And with these provisions, there seems also to be ascertained a re-arrangement of lands and seas, such as to afford the maximum of accommodation for commercial progress, and the most favourable distribution of temperature for the health and comfort of nations. The Christian believer who looks on these arrangements from the eminence of faith, will easily apprehend other adaptations, which I cannot at present state, further than the suggestion of a high probability that in these arrangements, regard was had to the entire course of a plan coeval with the foundation of the world.

I should add to this statement that all the traditions and ancient records of human history, together with the most trustworthy authorities on the structural remains and monuments of the globe—Cuvier, Lyell, and Buckland, with other scientific authorities—unite in fixing the origin of the human race at or near the period, to be approximately ascertained from a chronological mean. And when we compare the laws of human progress, as indicated by experience and history, with all that can be certainly ascertained of the beginnings of art and science, —laws, institutions, commerce, and the origins of empire—all seems to offer as full confirmation as probable inference can ask.

The various elements of the social state, slow in their development, complex in combination, and widely distinct in causal and local conditions, were, according to the known method of Him who, from eternity, hath "worked hitherto," gradually evolved through periods of duration, vast to finite conception, though little in the scope of duration that has no essential limit. When all was prepared in the succession of the stages of the eternal design, man and the train of living things subject to man, were placed on the destined scene, to run similarly a course of periods through an ascending series of social changes. Of this progress I shall have to say much in my next discourse.

But we may find confirmation not less strong, when we take into account the endowments of the creature for whom such large preparation was made—himself "fearfully and wonderfully made"—created manifestly in the image of his Maker—*a mind—a contriver and organizer*—endowed with moral affections, the capacities of love, pity, justice—capable of ascending in thought to the conception of virtue, of God, of a future state, and, *if* true to the archetypal standard, to realize a distant reflexion of Divinity. That his actual state falls far short, remains to be accounted for by any religion claiming to be true.

But it is enough for *this argument* to observe the endowments by which he has obtained the dominion over land and sea, and all that lives; his wide spread application of means to ends; his conversion of every element to his uses. It is no mere inference from authority to quote the language of my text as a description of what man is; "Let us make man in our own image, and after our likeness, and let him have dominion over the fish of the sea, and over the fowl of the air, and over the cattle." The comparison of man with God, in this highest conception of man, however warranted by authority, cannot be lightly, or without the deepest reverence, permitted. The Mind which holds within its grasp of operation all that lies within the Infinite and Eternal—to which the solar system is no more than the meanest piece of mechanism is to human skill, cannot be measured by any standard of human thought or language. But the specific indications are enough to place man in the assigned rank of earthly superiority.

It is not less within the scope of this argument, to recal many considerations and facts, which go to prove that man must have been in the beginning of his course of progress, instructed by his Creator. Whether this was effected by spiritual or direct communication, or by angelic ministry, it is nothing to our purpose to inquire; but such is the conclusion not to be evaded by any probable reasoning. Much, indeed, has this almost self-evident truth been obscured by the speculative ingenuity of theorists, ancient and modern, who, as usual with this class of thinkers, think it necessary to shew how all things have their origin, without calling Divine interposition to their aid; and ever find a strange facility in the assumption that any explanation must be sufficient in the absence of experimental fact. Such were the theories of Smith and Warburton, on language; of legal theorists, on the origin of the social contract and social institutions. On these curious fallacies I may not here enter in detail; but I trust that a brief examination of their general result will sufficiently expose the false principle. It will be more to the point to prove the contrary than to wade knee-deep in a mire of fallacies—of which the refutation can establish nothing. We cannot shew *how* God instituted social progress; but we can easily shew, that it was as much his work as the physical creation of man or man's world. To the speculative philosopher, I may just suggest, that no *law* of development, or of origination, which cannot be now actually discovered in effective operation, can be reasonably assumed to explain anything.

Among the various tribes of the brute creation, there are *existing* instincts, which govern their earliest movements from the womb, the shell, or the spawn, fully sufficient for all, or nearly all, the stages of their existence. There is an originating principle instilled in their very creation; their habits of life are essential elements of their nature. In man there is a nearly total absence of those conservative provisions: he is made to be tended, taught, and disciplined to the use of his faculties; such is his nature. He has no natural intuitive language, no instinctive knowledge of food, or of the means to supply the wants of his animal nature; of these, there is no indication, nor any authentic ground for the assumption that they ever were. He could, in his beginning, only have lived so long as starvation takes to kill; unless first taught by some of those methods, so obviously in the power of Him who has created all that is known. Nothing in living nature is so helpless as an infant; but if we suppose, as we must, that man was first framed in maturity of form and mind, there is surely no unreasonable stretch in the assumption, that he was further prepared for life, by the *same means* (though by a different method) as are still essential to his existence. It is easy to understand, and to a moderate extent, allow for the theoretic taste which aims at scientific uniformity in the exposition of nature, and would therefore resort to the easy expedient of explaining the phenomena of human nature and history on principles strictly entomological. But like all such plenary methods it is superficial and grossly fallacious. There are no points of analogy—the generic differences are too wide. The known, existing nature of man is, to be prepared by instruction for the entire course of his existence—all, at least, beyond what he is, in common with the dullest of the brute creation. No instinct is known for the development of his proper condition as man. From all that can be known, or in any way ascertained, he must have been from the beginning, as he still is, the subject of instruction: this is the special property of his nature—indispensable now, and therefore to be concluded so from the first. And for this essential process, there can be but one probable instrumentality.

But for this conclusion, the chain of historic deduction is not less strong. Such a view is far too comprehensive for the limit which I must here preserve; I may but sum it briefly. A retrospective view of human progress, as represented in history, or to be extracted from all tradition, leads to ages of social infancy—the rude beginnings of the structure of civilization—with all the certainty which the present argument requires. All the more complex and refined arts, sciences, modes of opinion, government and law, which constitute the body of civil society, are stamped with the record of a late beginning. The law of human progress is strictly a law of accelerative augmentation; that is to say, of new combinations from old; increasing with their depth, complexity, and number. If we follow such an order reversely, there must appear a descending order, leading to a state, in which we must recognize the pristine form, or simple elementary condition, from which any progress could reasonably be assumed to begin. Of such a state the elements must needs have been the work of Divine communication. From utter ignorance, there is no advance; for such there is no provision either in human nature, or in any circumstance which may be assumed in the sceptic theory. We have full sufficient experimental proof, not only in the general course of all trustworthy history; but there are, within living experience, examples *of every stage of human progress*, from the savage whose mind cannot pass beyond the scope of his animal cravings, up to the sage who can settle all questions by the magic of a theory. From the large compass of instances thus within the reach of observation, it may be affirmed, that, up to a certain stage of progress, the tendency of mankind has been to degenerate rather than to advance.

In the well known instances of savage races, some facts are clearly ascertained—there has not been found to exist any trace of those originating instincts to which might be traced the origin of a more advanced condition—while there has still appeared, more or less, the existence of certain primary elements of a degree of refinement far beyond their actual state, and a capability of receiving instruction, slowly enough to show how unlikely would be all chance of spontaneous advance. These primary elements have not been accounted for by tradition or theory—the efforts of theory fail in the first step; and, by their singular extravagance, mark the hopelessness of such efforts. Language—letters—with the elementary notions of religion and of spiritual being, may be taken as examples.

On the whole, it appears in the highest degree probable, that the origin of social arts and social progress must be sought in the very origin of the human race, and ascribed to the immediate instrumentality of the same will and power. This, independent of all theory, is the most probable, and has all the characters of a matter of course; it is encumbered with no difficulty that does not equally effect the very origin of man, whose very existence in his pristine state cannot otherwise be explained. The refined analysis of modern philosophy is hardly competent to expound the subtle combination of those primitive elements which have been ascribed to the rudest stages of the human intellect—the language—the letters—the prime elements of law and theology.*

On the strength of these considerations, which I cannot now further expand, I think it not unreasonable to infer that the primary elements of civilization—the first rudiments of the arts of life—of communication—with all that respects the recognized relations between man and God, admit but of one explanation—the same by which alone the origin of man himself can be intelligibly derived.

I have not now adverted to the moral and intellectual structure of the human mind, which are very clearly applicable to the point at present under consideration, as I shall have to enforce them in several aspects in further steps of this enquiry. But I may here call your attention to the observable fact, that according to any received theory the human mind is a very peculiar instance of a complex and systematic structure, framed in relation to

* Note A.

the sphere of its existence, the provisions for its varied wants and functions, and the destiny it has achieved. Its powers, attainments, inventions, the moral, political, and religious structures which—like the coraline islands,—it has raised from the depths of unfathomed antiquity, place it within the same theory of design and preconceived purpose, as already stated.

On the strength of these considerations, which could be greatly enforced by more full and specific details, it may be safely affirmed, and this without any allowance for its divine authority, that the sense of the passage from Genesis is literally descriptive of the place man fills in this world; and on the same grounds it is plainly to be inferred that—so far as can be probably judged from the actual condition and endowments of man, as well as from all the dispositions of the scene in which he holds so manifestly the chief place and dominion, and occupies all its operative elements and natural resources—he must in reason be regarded as designed for this place of vantage and earthly supremacy; and therefore is to be considered as the main object of the arrangements and provisions which are so made to work together for his benefit. Finally, that he is to be regarded as the object of the main purpose of Him who is the source and Sovereign Disposer of the whole. Whether the design, thus so far accomplished, is to be regarded as sufficient in itself and final, or a step towards a further end, remains to be considered—and of what nature this end may be. The question which next arises in order is this, what in probability appears to be the main end or purpose of God in the creation of man. This I purpose to discuss in the

3*

two following lectures:—I will now only state the main division under which it will be conveniently pursued. All the theories I know of, may be resolved generally into two, which will be found to comprize every condition of the enquiry: these I shall class under the terms social and spiritual. The first to include some state of ultimate social perfection—the second some theory of a future state after death. Of each, the varieties may be very many; but they must respectively offer some common conditions, and the alternative, when once attained, may be further submitted to the same tests of probable enquiry.

And now, in conclusion, allow me to offer a reflection, somewhat more immediately practical, which my first proposition suggests.

We who are here this morning assembled, in the presence of Him who is nowhere absent, happily possess a faith settled on foundations far surer than any inferences from such arguments as can be brought in opposition to either natural unbelief, or philosophical fallacy. But there is a lesson to the heart, as well as to the reason, in such considerations as may appear to substantiate our vital connexion with the great Author of our being, and our inseparable comprehension in the main purpose of so many and such vast and complex arrangements. If we look into our own consciousness, and reflect how far we are in spirit conformable to the purpose so amply corroborated, the reflection will convey no lesson of pride. But it may well expose the rash reliance of some, upon the presumed forbearance or mercy which would acquiesce in the frustration of all the conditions of a main design, so often and so fully and peremptorily declared. To be comprehended in a scheme, vast enough to fill eternity, and precise as the power and wisdom of its Author can compass, and yet to be found wanting, is the awful condition of those in whose hearts and lives there is nothing more than a formal and desultory recognition of that which in the sight of Him who is the arbiter of man's destiny must be the very end and purpose of his existence. This is not merely the conclusion of a curious theory, but an awful reality—not a thesis for doctrinal learning, or form for formal compliance, but a fact, to each of us the most momentous—for a few passing years concealed from the unbeliever, by the shadows which he pursues, but to be inevitably disclosed by an event which happens once to all men. When he who lives in vain—whose whole life is a violation of the intent of his God—must stand before that awful Being to be judged, not according to the world's law of opinion—or by the rationalist's theory—or his own assumptions of freedom from earthly crime—or by pharisaical dogmas of ritual conformity—or by good deeds done for the reward of human praise, or for the benefit from worldly prudence; but according to the purpose ordained, and the conditions declared.

There is happily yet another side of this same object of contemplation, if sincerely entertained. It brings to view the Author of all the great and beneficent provisions of nature, as one having a main interest in us—a great purpose in which we are essentially involved. And while we see and understand the vast skill and wisdom, and the boundless power displayed in the visible indications of this purpose, the heart is led to a more thorough sense of the probable magnitude and glorious realization of those promises, which are to be the completion of a design so magnificently commenced and provided for, and a nearer estimate of those expectations which we look for.

I need not, I am sure, add, that in this practical application I do not mean to lessen the value of a lesson, far more obvious, and far nearer to the Christian heart— the evidence of the great sacrifice, once offered for us.

LECTURE II.

"Thou turnest man to destruction; again thou sayest, Come again ye children of men."---PSALMS, XC. 3.

We have now, I trust on grounds of very high probability, arrived at the two conclusions; first, that the Creator of this world must have had a distinct purpose or final end in view; and secondly, we have deduced the claim of the human race to be considered as the main object of this purpose. Our next step must be to inquire, on grounds similarly ascertainable, what this purpose may presumably be. The ultimate end of the Creator is probably very far beyond the utmost grasp of man's unassisted reason. Still, from the careful comparison of all that is open to our observation, some satisfactory general conclusions as to its true character may be obtained; whether, for instance, it is to end in the present life and social state of man, or, as revealed religion affirms, is to terminate in some future state after death. To these alternatives, I have already observed that all theories worth consideration may be reduced.

Of the two assumptions thus defined, I must now proceed to examine the first or social assumption. In this inquiry, using the term social in its largest sense to include all opinions or theories, in which this present life or any state of man it may comprehend, is assumed to be his ultimate destination.

Before I can proceed satisfactorily, I must call on the

reader to keep in view a very important distinction, by which the conditions of this inquiry must be limited in its application. The social alternative is affected by some very evident considerations which are inapplicable to the other. In the assumption of the future state, as implied in the spiritual theory, we should have to deal with the unknown, with a futurition not in any degree within the compass of any experience we have before us; in probability conditions without name or precedent, belonging to the infinite and eternal of being, only bounded within the scope of unconceived possibility; and consequently, while it is allowable to draw probable inferences from every indication we can positively discover, it does not equally follow that we can argue from the absence of any indication that human reason or experience may require. In any reasonable contemplation of a probable future state of man, we have before us a vast compass of possibility beyond conception or conjecture, to which all we know or can conceive is too small for comparison; and considering this little as only preparatory to that which is to follow, and having with it unknown relations, our inferences from even the facts or history of religion itself must offer little ground for certain inference. Somewhat preceding in the eternal past, or to be hereafter; something in the nature and destination of man, or in the divine law, or in the attributes of Deity—might account (if known) for facts or doctrines which may seem irrelevant or even inconsistent.

Now, on the contrary, after allowing for the narrow limit of man's knowledge of that which he knows best, the elements and the operative conditions of the social state, together with the theoretic completion towards which all its tendencies seem to advance, are fully within the grasp of reason and experience. So far as it is fairly open to reason, the social destiny of man is to be accomplished by *known* instrumentalities; if any further instrumentalities have been made known, they belong to the opposite alternative.

So far being understood, the following conditions may be unreservedly applied to any theory which implies the *finality* of the present state.

According to any reasonable version of socialism, having *known* realities for its foundation, there can be no allowable escape from the field of experience; we can admit no completion but that conformable to known tendencies. But with this we have to admit what has been clearly proved, the boundless power and wisdom which, whatever may be the design, have been the contriving and conducting instruments.

With a plan so limited, instrumentalities so known, and power so vast, there appears no ground for the assumption of any obstacle or material interruption. God cannot be presumed to have wavered in a main design, or permitted the wheel of progress to go astray. The plan must have uniformly proceeded without any interruption, unaccountable on its known conditions, or such as to show a deviation or total cessation of its operative machinery. The governing intelligence must have been cognizant of all its movements, watching at all its periods, and this without such interruption as to be unaccountable but by some departure from the destined course, or to be explained only by some other theory;

for we must bear in mind (under the present assumption), we speak simply of God as the author of nature, and as a Power all whose operations are characterized by the utmost uniformity of operation and the most uninterrupted efficiency; nor is it to be lost sight of that we are engaged with the assumption of the *social system*, as a main and final design.

Under these conditions nothing is to be allowed for failure, accident, or contrary workings, or the absence of any of the known essential elements which the progress of the plan should require, and the care of its author supply.

It may further, in the second place, be required, that on due examination the proposed completion should not be found to fall miserably short of the previous arrangements which are matters of observation, and of the power and wisdom employed upon it. Of the boundless presence of this Power in every point of space, there is evidence in the all-pervading life with which every spot of nature teems, and the inexhaustible variety of beautiful conceptions and skilful organizations vast beyond, and minute beneath, the grasp of mortal sense, all, perfection in plan and operative precision.

Now, when these considerations are strictly applied to the assumption of finality in the plan and completion of human progress, there must evidently appear a total want of that continuity of progress and of that efficient conduct of periods and processes of advance which should, *in conformity with the assumption*, be expected. I shall not, I trust, be supposed in the slightest degree to question the universal control of Divine Providence in any period of time, or change of human concerns. This I assume, and the assumption is implied in the very ground of my argument, that God must be uninterruptedly present through all time and place, and as much so in the remotest wild where the foot of man has never trod, as in the heart of London. But what I would now press is a fact manifested through the records of every age and nation, the utter absence of all indications reconcilable with the supposed finality. I cannot find the essential provisions, nor is there discernible one unquestionable step of the required advance towards the consummation proposed—that is, towards a social frame and constitution, bearing any tendency to or proportion with the assumed conditions, or, indeed, with any result which any theory could fix upon as deserving the term of completion, on whatever standard. I do not mean to deny, but on the contrary feel entirely convinced, that the present state of man bears some settled relation to the entire system of the Divine arrangements, so far as they include his final destination: I assume all we can see to be a portion of one great whole. But this does not concern the actual question in hand. There is to be observed the plain distinction between that which is *subsidiary* and that which is to be the *complete result*. If the generally assumed conditions of the best reasoned social theories were the means to be adopted for such an end as must be so implied, there is no probable reason why the assumed completion of social progress should not have been reached four thousand years ago, by the uninterrupted application of the moral, political, and economical means already applied, and shown to have had efficient influence in the promotion of civilization. Very little attentive reflection will be sufficient to perceive that (considering all civilizing influences known or alleged,) their real and efficient operation has actually been confined to short periods of time, and this chiefly within the few last centuries.

Look but for one moment on the general aspect of the world's past, as it is to be seen in all we know of history. I do not now speak of the recondite and doubtful matter of learned antiquarianism, but of the general consent of record and tradition, in every form, in the consent of all authority. What has been the actual course of civilization? In a slow progression of 4,000 years (to fix a period,) it has been smouldering dimly, upon the verge of extinction ever; it has migrated through every latitude from the tropic to the polar circle, always leaving behind barbarism and desolation; from the river of Ulai to the Nile and the Ganges—scenes long abandoned by progress—where all but the human spirit, bears witness to the magnificence of creation; down to the four great empires which, each in its turn, claimed earth's dominion, and seemed to approach the socialist's earthly ideal, and, in turn, left a lesson of the vanity of earthly things, but added little to the foundations of social progress; until we come to periods which, however they may end, plainly indicate within what narrow periods art, science, manners, and all the laws and institutions of civilized life might advance, if the true foundations were laid, had such been the purpose designed from the first. The social theorist, (let me recal,) so far as he is entitled to present notice, proceeds on clear and fully known conditions, to an ascertained result; he cannot, as in the case of an unknown and unimaginable future, take refuge in the plea of unknown possibilities emanating from other non-existent conditions, and more universal laws of being; he is bound by the conditions included within his proposed completion. The progress towards his vision of social perfection, has through long periods run a short course. In the vast compass of the everlasting future, a plan of wider comprehension and more high and spiritual conditions may be insisted upon, in which any present interruption or seeming obstacle may be of no consideration, or nothing more in comparison than a grain of sand to the globe of the earth. But, on the present assumption, such breaches of continuity would amount to frustration; they must indicate either the unallowable assumption that providence has for long periods neglected its great primary intent, or that the progress thus intermitted, has relation to some further and different consummation, to the purposes of which it is exclusively conducted in its pauses, advances, and transitions.

It would be vain, and, in the present argument, needless, to go minutely and at a length of detail which our time cannot admit of, into the traditionary periods of time, to prove what no student of antiquity doubts; the long ages of human barbarism or degeneracy, the retardations and retrogressions of the earliest known peoples and empires, the long stagnation in the slow advances of the nations of latter times. I will not speak of Goth, and Hun, and Vandal, and the greatest empire of which there is any record, trampled into ruin, because such was manifestly the adopted means in the transition to a nobler civilization, a great restoration. But the dawn of that day was tedious, and laden with moral and physical pestilence; the vapors of the infernal world seem to have gained the ascendant. The approach of modern civilization seemed for many generations like the setting in of a long, and dark, and stormy night; and if the Christian philosopher can discern a higher hand ruling these tempestuous times to brighter ends, it is as evident that if earthly progress *alone* were to be advanced—if any blessing merely secular which our times have experience of were simply the end of attainment, there was no assignable need for all those wasteful retardations, those disgraceful and bloody transitions, of which, in most instances, the horror and suffering was far beyond any compensating advantage. It is, indeed, too obvious to be omitted, that when we look more critically into the best known of those terrible changes, which did so little for the secular progress of mankind, other ends of another nature seem to have been forwarded, so as to suggest a far different end in the contemplation of Providence; but, surely, little marked by the uniformity and unity either of means or results which are essential to the theory now under our consideration. Those means of progress, if we are to regard them as such—those exterminations, those obliterations of arts, and morals, and sciences— those great imperial ruins might have, many of them, been spared, and all they effected, been compressed into a twelfth of the time. More has been done for art and knowledge and human progress since Kepler and Galileo, than through all the lengthened ages of the past. It is still more apparent that, within the existing generation, more of social progress has been attained than in the whole of the preceding time; and, in the event, the proposed completion is as far off as ever; I may be allowed, perhaps, to add, still more obviously unattainable, as we reach to higher points. However this may appear, I may, I trust, be permitted to affirm of the past history of man that it indicates neither the method, the uniformity, nor continuity to be looked for from a competent intelligence, keeping in view its own main and exclusive ends. The courses of the world bear no proportion to the theory of a *primary* purpose; they are to be characterized as a succession of remotely scattered movements, seemingly more contrived to arrest and defeat the ends of Providence, only repelled and turned to good by a high overruling aim, than adopted as means to final ends. Such an order of events may have been permitted for ends beyond human conjecture, but manifestly do not indicate the conduct of a main and final plan of social perfection in this present state.

But of the past I have said enough; let us come to what we know on experience. We have, to some extent, to deal with great popular illusions; which, in whatever degree they may really affect the faith of mankind, form the entire substratum of such theories as are here to be discussed. First, there is very widely entertained, a loose and false estimate of what social perfection is, and what it requires; and secondly, if not portion of the same error, a disregard of the enormous obstacles and defects in the provisions for such an end. Among those who have stated their views in conformity with such an expectation, the progress and intent of humanity is seldom, if ever, regarded beyond the advance of social order, either towards a perfection of the civil constitution of nations, or the completion of some vision of human prosperity. Of the wealth of nations, the advances of knowledge, the improved intercourse of nations, and the like, little need be said. I am quite ready to grant a large scope for the reasonable speculations of the philanthropist; I can set no bounds to the splendid triumphs of science, or the wonderful advance of material improvements in art.

But for the end proposed, far other conquests are to be achieved. The general amount of human knowledge, and the imposing fabric of civil order, with its controlling machinery of laws and institutions, and the embodied accumulations of opinion and feeling which cast their shadowy influence over the whole, impress the imagination with the *prestige* of a mighty power, and impart a venerable aspect to this temporal state of things in which man "walketh in a vain shadow." In the noise and glare of the vast mechanism of our social state, the visionary theorist loses sight of the individual character and inner nature in which his grand theory is lost; and yet no dream can be more plainly illusive.

A man may live in times of great light, and still be very dark in himself—like a blind man in the blaze of day,—he may possess all knowledge, and lack all wisdom; he may be a moral theorist, and devoid of goodness; he may possess all comforts and not be happy. It is not in these, that virtue, happiness, or wisdom consist. If these could achieve the social dream, the world should be at its noon of perfection long ago. But the mechanism of locomotion may interfuse the commonwealth of nations, and man stand still, and this fair globe continue to be drenched with blood, and communities to be disturbed by social outrage. The starry deep may be guaged far into infinity; geology may grave its dates upon the primeval granite, and chemistry have left no element uncontrolled; the electric chain may "waft a sigh from Indus to the Pole;" all Europe may be rounded into the liberty of the communist's dream of peace and freedom, and man (the lord of this world's estate, the favoured creature of God,) still remain what he is yet known to be, until his nature itself undergoes an essential and elementary change—that inborn change which no earthly school can impart. Should such a change come over his nature, it must come immediate from the same Spirit that first moulded man from the dust of earth, and breathed into his nostrils the breath of life. Such a change has, at best, no place in this argument; in a certain sense we may admit its possible realization, but it is not here to be assumed. In fact, if all known social elements and every assumption of the most transcendental rationalism be fairly analyzed, in the whole, whether of known fact or visionary fiction, there will be found not one efficient element of the assumed social state—no provision for the social theory of perfection, unless one which the alternative under present consideration excludes. Though it is worthy of note, that some of the theories of modern socialism have made an unconscious admission of the Christian principle, in the adoption of the fundamental element of universal charity, by any merely social working unattainable; thus affirming an effect of which the cause is excluded, the modern socialist has been driven to borrow a page from the evangelist, strangely coupling his unattainable panacea with a theory of licentious morals and manners—not, indeed, quite absurdly ; he could in no other way evade the vices, than by the disguise of a name, by "calling evil good, and good evil." Such is the morality of the sceptic, and the logic of his philosophy.

This leads to the essential impediment in the way of all the most seemingly reasonable theories of any social perfection, which depends exclusively on the existing elements of humanity, or which takes for granted the moral perfectibility of man. Let us first see what is implied in such theories, when least discordant from the most admitted principles of social order. We cannot claim less than the cessation of the prevalent 'misdirection of human tendencies, which degrade, pervert, and disturb every nation. We should expect the universal bond of peace and charity among neighbours and peoples; a rest from contention over the habitable globe ; no self-centred despotisms, no popular insubordinations, no leading into captivity, nor complainings in our streets, no fraud, no extortion, no hate, no wrong ambition. Where in the home, or the street, or the senate, or the council, are these things to be found ? The apostle of socialism, under whatever denomination, has—though with sad adulterations—promised something of the kind. But what specific has he found for the innate root, the inborn nature of man, of which moral evil and social disorder are the bitter fruit ? How will he contrive to make " the evil tree bring forth good fruit ?" Has he not, in the transcendental attic where such dreams haunt the theoretic pillow, wholly lost sight of human life—the craving and imperious passions, appetites, and desires which compose the natural man—foaming ever over all the bars of prudence, overwhelming the very restraints of the individual self-interest of which they are the component objects? What earthly motive will be found to root these strong elements out of life?

If any one, in his inexperience of the actual world, imagines that he can, in either its present state or advancing progress, discover the slightest indication of this bright solution—as visionary as the *Saturnia Regna* of the ancient poet—I would beg of him to turn a moment's thoughtful attention to the full-blown civilization of London or Paris, where over-ripeness seems verging towards decay. In these great centres of every moral force, where the means and appliances of life, where human intelligence and every influence which belongs to the economy of man's civil state or social progress, are at their maximum of power; what, beneath the bright and imposing surface of things, is the reality? See if it has made even a remote approach toward the social end you would seek from the Creator of this magnificent frame of nature. I do not propose any comparison with a spiritual theory; such, when proposed, has its own solution to offer. I now propose only what the most sceptical philosophy which admits anything, must admit—a glorious standard of perfect order, the visible frame of creation. How the aspect of our proudest civilization, if looked to as a worthy end, sinks in the comparison; how little, so compared, does it bear the aspect of an original design.

So far from this, as our civil and social advances in knowledge and its material results become more rapidly accelerated from year to year, there is no progress whatever in that moral advance, which is indispensable in any theory which relies on social influences or states of human perfection ; and I may add, it is not only true, as I have endeavoured to show, that both in its progress and constitution the social state wants the character of final intent, but that it is sensibly deficient in those characters which might indicate *permanency ;* I might indeed, not without strong grounds, say, those conditions of a further progress, in any sense worthy of the name. But such a position would involve me in controversy beyond the need of my inquiry, and the subject is one upon which I must touch very lightly ; it has many sore points, and the probable truth is little in harmony with many of our habitual prepossessions. I shall offer but this one suggestion. In all the real advances of social progress there are tendencies which, while they tend to accelerate its advances, are yet such that they cannot pass beyond a certain level, much less attain a theoretical maximum, without the development of other tendencies from the depths of human nature, such as to shake the whole existing structure of society. Such developments are fully exemplified in history, and are largely involved in revolutionary changes, and in the decline and fall of states. Nor are such indications wanting among the signs of the present time.[*] In this, not unlike every other transitory thing, the most flourishing states may

---

[*] Note C.

be shown to have contained, in their day of strongest life, a germination of the seeds of death; diseases springing from their sources of strength. Examples are familiar.

In the diffusion of wealth, for instance, and of that civil equality which the social theory requires; there may be conceived a stage of advance in these essential respects, which, unless the animal passions and far more expansive and socially influential moral vices inherent in man, could be at the same time, *pari passu*, abated, could not fail to lead to the most disastrous results. The social theorist often leans upon assumptions, respecting the influence of popular education, which are supported by no experience. Ambition, selfishness, covetousness, insane speculation, party delusion, false reasoning and vicious aims, fill the heart of the sage and the simple alike: the aim may be different, but the wider scope and more alert faculty is stronger for evil as well as for good, and mostly far more so inclined. There is in the mere advance of popular knowledge, exalting as it may in theory be, nothing essentially reformative; and I may here be allowed to borrow the language, at least, of a higher philosophy. "Though I have the gift of prophecy and understand all mysteries, and all knowledge, though I have all faith, so that I could remove mountains, and have not charity, I am nothing." I quote these words because, without resting on their authority, they convey the whole truth, as much in a philosophical and merely secular sense, as in the more spiritual meaning of the Apostle. With another ancient sage, we may truly say, "In much wisdom, there is much folly;" in the results of *mere* intellectual cultivation, the age abounds with examples of this, that they are often but mere amplifications of folly. One philosophy alone contains the germ of moral perfection—and this, though manifestly and most practically reformative according to its own implied intent, was yet not designed to satisfy the condition of socialism, nor likely to be so far applied; but this I shall notice further on, it is not directly within the scope of the present question. The law of a Divine institution, whatever might be its universal influence, if universally applied, is not practically the governing law of conduct, feeling, and public opinion, nor the actuating spirit of what the socialist, or even the world of nominal Christians would term progress. To pronounce what social life and the moral tone of the world might become, under the dominion of such a faith as is professed in our country at least, is unhappily not within the scope of probable expectation; some higher and purer spirit, some interposition of a will higher, and a wisdom more true than is in the councils of princes, or the representatives of peoples, must descend amongst us to cleanse and assuage the turbid and troubled waters of life. What, in a potential or theoretic sense, might be the real influence of this spiritual interposition, shall be considered when it comes under our notice, as a main alternative of the question under discussion.

Let us now take a passing glnce upon the actual state of man in this present enlightened period. We have, far within the short period of three score and ten, allotted to human life, arrived at an unprecedented stage of advance; and, not to repeat my admissions of the vast and wonderful conquests of art and science—there seems to be a not less wide and rapid diffusion of popular intelligence—the clown seems treading fast upon the courtier's heels, and every trade growing into something of a learned profession—the "schoolmaster" has been now long "abroad"—a sower (not identical with him of the parable), has scattered his seeds, by roadside and rural recess, in every corner of the land. The result is easy to read. All the strongholds of order and authority in every civilized land have been shaken and are tottering. Old customary restraints of opinion, the safeguards of institution are dissolved: old wheels and springs of rule worn, deadlocked, and beginning to be cast aside as useless; and new, not discoverable. In brief—a social phase, which (without meaning to refer to any higher solution) seems itself suggestive of the close and catastrophe of the great secular drama of humanity: an end differing widely from that proposed by social Platonism. Anxious as I have been, to repress the strong and perhaps extreme suggestions, which the subject of this discourse forces upon us, it is impossible wholly to look with ordinary sobriety of regard, on the slow but hardly doubtful gathering storms that seem growing over the civilized world. The portentous shadows of some disastrous day—casting gloom and apprehension over nations—afflicting monarchs with "fear of change."

But I gladly relieve you from this topic of gloomy mystery. Let me ask your attention to a different and more entirely practical and experimental aspect of this sage theory, which must equally apply in every form it can take, within the bounds of reason. Human happiness is the great final aim of the socialist's theory. So far as he has any practical meaning, he promises a glorious millennium of peace, order, and contentment, when philosophy shall be the God of this world, and human nature casting aside control, shall revel in unchained freedom; when the law shall no longer sit above the philosophic communist; or the palace overshadow the cottage; or the soil be appropriated by the wealthy few; but equal rights and privileges maintain the wide and peaceful level of a rational equality—resting upon the philosophic sense of all mankind—when knowledge shall cover the earth "as the waters cover the sea." Such is the ultimate extreme of the social philosophy. But, not to dwell upon the fact that we have had an experimental illustration of this bright dream, not seventy years ago, and know the result, an awful lesson to the social reformer, let us cast one more glance on the realities of human nature, and judge how far such theories can have any place in the design of man's creation, such as may appear from the indications of nature and observed reality.

With endowments and capabilities worthy of the place he holds in the known scale of living things; such as fully to bear out higher expectations than any social theory will dare to expect; what, at best, is the sum of his earthly allotment? What, under any assumption, limited to this life, can it be? Can the social theorist deny the Hebrew poet's affecting complaint, "Verily, man walketh in a vain shadow, and disquieteth himself in vain; he heapeth up riches, and cannot tell who shall gather them." Human life is written over with contradictions to every social theory of perfection. Every human path is crossed by the tracks of death; its painful records are in every house—the scars of remembrance as life goes on, accumulate on every heart. Two thirds of that little time, which—according to the statistics of mortality—can be the lot of but few, are lost in the waste of infancy and the painful imbecility of old age, when " man's strength is labor and sorrow, so soon passeth it away and he is gone." Does it not seem strange insanity, that such a life should be the socialist's dream of rest?

But the illusion of this state of being is well worth a moment's pause. We are liable to be imposed upon by the spacious magnitude of our world; its systems of order, power, and rule; the sway of opinion; the aggregate of interests and aggregate of life, all magnified by our individual dependence, and still more by our blindness to the vastitudes beyond; all filling the whole mind, shut in by its narrow circle of vision. All beyond is as the starry universe: to the dweller of the little field of our atom globe, non-existent in contemplation. In this transitory being we see only what comes out into its sunshine—youth and manhood and the onward flowing affections of the rushing current of our days. Pain and poverty and sorrow are shrouded in their dim retreats; sickness goes aside to die; death hides in the last concealments of mortality. The outer world glides by, like a broad river shining in the sun, and rippled in the healthful breeze; loaded with the pleasure barque and commercial sail. Ever passing to the deep—yet ever full.

Suppose—with this faithful picture on your minds—the brightest lot, any theory of earthly perfection, any dream of happiness worthy of this creature of our theory. And consider well what can be its real amount; if it is to be so cut short, so limited in attainment, and —for it belongs to the social theory—so to end in the blank void of annihilation. Such is the creed that contains no promise of, no warrant for, a future hope. If there remains nothing after the toil and troubled course of life, its many trials and still contracting circle of communion, to console the sequestered endurance of old age, when its solitude is haunted by the shadow of the coffin and the shroud—the worm and the dust—and the next wave of mortality visibly swelling over its head: when the contemporary generation has gone by, and that which follows is now ready to tread over its dust—to trample out the memory of its name—and if the mind still holds its office,—if thought remains clear, and man at last has but the dregs of the exhausted cup —the memory of many sorrows—for life can be prolonged upon no other condition—surely if this, at best, be all for which God made man, it is but a sad delusion, a grievous falling off from the magnificent provision— the splendid endowment—the imperial domain of land and sea—the gorgeous fabric of life, and its broad social structure. Whether we pass in review the individual— passing like a brief light across the narrow circle of life's day in which he moves—or the empire, but a little more slowly disappearing into the dimness of tradition, as little remembered as a morning cloud, and leaving a long wake of darkness behind;—leaving a name to what we call history, and a desert on some unfrequented shore—Babylon or Tadmor in the wilderness: the dull echo from the tomb, and the mouldering pillar, which give the true reply to the socialist's high-sounding, though essentially low and senseless expectation.

This slight sketch of man's present state might be heightened much by considerations, which will come in more fitly in a further step of our inquiry. But, on the strength of these facts, which no mortal may deny—the trite echo of all time, the low murmur of the stream of ages—I might ask the advocate of the social creed, who rejects the consolation of a better, will he insist that it is full compensation that he may travel faster, fare better, or amass more quickly; and tread on still in the same brief circle of sin, endeavour, and disappointment, closed by infirmity and ending without hope. Surely, the All-wise Giver of life and mind, of hopes and affections, never designed so palpable an abortion, to fill man's imperial place in the magnificent harmony of His great creation. How emphatically might we apply the apostle's comment on the same assumption—the socialism of the ancient gnostic: "If in this life only we have hope in Christ, we are of all men most miserable." It will suggest itself to most of my hearers, that the intent of this passage was not precisely that to which it is here applied; it was applied to all who renounced the pomps and vanities, the imaginary goods of life, for Christ and His sake. But it is, in principle, as true in the sense of these statements, and suggests a further apt truth. How much all that, in any true sense, is called goodness, must be supposed to imply self-denial, the resignation of pleasures and advantages, on the ground of justice and the social welfare—how much of what is called virtue, the perfection of the social state would require—what regard for all, what abnegation of self. Now, consider this as it respects the social theory, and what must be the result? If this present state were "the be all and end all," the best and noblest minds were nothing more than a more deep illusion, a darker frustration—"of all men most miserable"—well might folly laugh, and sin say to virtue: "Let us eat and drink, for to-morrow we die."

Now, the socialist's theory may be put into a summary interrogation, to which the answer will be a useful illustration of much of the preceding remarks, and an apt conclusion for the present step of this inquiry. "Do you mean," he may ask, "to affirm that the Providence to whom the Christian ascribes the changes of the world, and a constant vigilance for five or six thousand years in the conduct of a great design, has been all this time exerting a waste of force, of time and means, and, through all changes, building up a massive fabric of social order—a deeply founded system of thought, language, law, custom, and civil rule—all to come to nothing? Will you assert that the progress, which you admit to be from the Creator of the world, is to stop short, retrograde, or dissolve, 'like the fabric of a vision,' when you admit its resources are at the highest?" Now, premising that this profound question is sufficiently answered already, the following illustration may be accepted as a summary view of that social theory I have set in opposition to the spiritual.

If a simple savage from some remote island unknown to civilization were to visit the civilized world, and, among others of its wonders, to be shown the arrangements of some great architectural work in progress of erection, partly shut in and concealed in its wooden enclosures, and covered from the eye in its unfashioned array of poles and ladders and scaffoldings, and surrounded by all the rubbishy detritus of waste material; the savage might stand amazed at the gigantic display of power, labour, and contrivance, and, like the social theorist in his ignorance, imagine some precise end of permanence in so vast seeming an expenditure of means and methods. It would be explained that such was not the true intent of these objects of his admiration; that the structure that so moved his wonder was but temporary, and to be taken down when its end was served. Within that unsightly mass (it might be said) which excites your ignorant admiration, there stands the true design of the architect, splendid and complete in its beautiful proportions and permanent structure, but only to be fully understood when the rubbish you are applauding shall be removed for ever. Such is the actual case. This temporal scene, wholly devoid of all indications of a final or permanent end, is yet needful for the conduct of a further design, from which imperfection, disorder, and viscissitude must, in conformity with all the ends of creation, be excluded.

It is not very long since an eminent apostle of socialism was allowed to give the fullest exposition of his views, and all that could be said to recommend them, in this very city. His argument had no real application to his own theory; but was an inadvertent admission of that which he would reject. He preached universal love as the great regenerating principle. And, on the strength of a pretended discovery—this piracy from truth—he promised a halcyon era to the world—a social millennium not incumbered with law or church. He soon discovered that he might as well preach to the winds, as speak Gospel morals separated from all that can enforce them, to the stormy passions and depravities of the world. We all know, and the social theorist saw clearly—for it is plain enough—that if the morals of the Gospel, the motives of faith, and the influence ascribed to a higher spirit than human could be realized without that faith, without that spirit—in opposition to the world's most confirmed and notorious tendencies great moral and social changes might still be not unreasonably looked for; just as man might fly if he were a bird, or any other change might be effected which nature has not made possible. It is thus the socialist's last refuge is an argument for the very alternative he rejects. On this ground alone I might ask for a decision. But this would be to omit much more valuable, because direct confirmation. The argument so far amounts but to the negation of one alternative; we have to see on what similar grounds the other is to be affirmed.

LECTURE III.

I see that all things come to an end, but thy commandment is exceeding broad.—Psalm cxix. 96.

IF we fairly consider the conditions applied to the former, or social alternative proposed for our discussion, it is plain that for the present part of our inquiry, they must be in some degree modified. In the former, we had to examine the theory of a scheme, of which (according to the hypothesis), both the means and end proposed are wholly under the inspection of reason. In the second, the means must be, for the greater part, mysterious, and the end still more so. The first may be compared to any complex mechanism of which the machinery and application are wholly within our use; the second, to that solar movement, of which the fact is known, but the path and governing centre, the past and future inscrutable. Religion, as connected with another state, beginning in the far past, and reaching into the future, may be liable to many undiscoverable conditions, only explicable by its essential relations with another vaster system of laws, policies, events, and ends, of which man, and all that concerns him, are but a little part.

Nevertheless, the very conditions of which I have shewn the failure, when applied to the former division of this inquiry, will appear to hold good in the history of religion; and this more precisely, in proportion as by proper limitations the inquiry becomes more close.

We have already seen the necessity of supposing man's first instruction to have been from his Creator. This conclusion, of itself, goes far to establish the high probability of an original relation between him and his Maker, amounting to religious affection and obedience. The observance of divine teaching and the recognition of God are the first elements of religion.

But that religion did exist from the earliest period that can be reached by human inquiry is not matter of question. It is traceable as the first element of government and civil order. Nor is it less to be proved from the history of the numerous superstitions and religious corruptions of the ancient world. In these we shall find both confirmations of no small inferential value, as well as some strongly urged but easily answered objections.

But, first, I must ask attention to one more extensive source of confirmation, one which I shall not now have time to do more than mention, but of which you will at once recognize the importance. The elementary constitution of man's moral nature, not only indicates the purpose for which he was "fearfully and wonderfully made," but even the very outline and main ethical characters of that purpose, and the scheme by which it should have been conducted. I now only advert to this general indication, as an easy key to the truth, which, at first application, must exclude all heathenism, as the essential conditions of a civilized moral system are wanting in all. The first instruction communicated to the parents of mankind must have been adapted, at least, to the true design—to the moral order of a race designed for a state of moral and spiritual advance. We cannot consistently assume the Author of nature, as known in all His works, to have proposed by means of imposture, to found systems of which the theory (at least) is grounded on truth, justice, and all the moral virtues. A religion from God must, consistently with our grounds of argument, essentially include the conditions of moral perfection. We thus exclude all heathen systems. The origin of divine worship cannot have recognized the bandit gods of Olympus, or the reptile worship of old Egypt, or the *nigra somnia* of Persian and Hindu fanaticism. Sober reason and common sense will spurn such revolting imputations against Him whose power and glory are witnessed in all we can see.

The multiplicity of these old superstitions has, with most pernicious effect, been advanced by a sophist of the Gallic revolutionary school,* as an objection against all religion. This fallacy has derived great force, from the universal tendency of ignorance to confound unlike things which bear a common name and pretension. When the objection is aimed *at all*, it seems needless to scrutinize their several claims; and yet nothing can be more plain than the grounds of an opposite inference, in the case of religion. So far from favouring the sceptical conclusion, the contrary is the plain inference of reason, from the mass of pagan corruptions for which an origin may vainly be sought until we find it in some primary faith. Now, waiving all allusion to doubted or disputed records, and looking simply to the changes of religion within historic memory, there may be

* Volney.

clearly identified a constant process, by which a true religion must become, in no long period, the source of many false. You have only to consult the records of the Christian churches for eighteen and a half centuries, to discern what human folly, abuse of reason, sentiment, and passion—what political intrigue and priestcraft working together can do. How the dreams of scholastic subtlety—the profane babblings " of science falsely so called "—or the chimeras of ascetic mysticism, can work upon a few clear and peremptory declarations of doctrine. The ancient sources of human aberration are not lost wholly to the world in these philosophic times. We need no refined theory to explain how these abortions of human wisdom grew—they are the weeds that spring at our feet. The wildest chimeras of Hindu superstition are (however monstrous and uncouth), not less reconcilable to reason and authority than much in worship and dogma with which the church history of civilized Europe makes us familiar; we shall not need, for this lesson, to grope among the tombs and catacombs of Thebes and ancient Memphis, or " call antiquity from the old schools of Greece." No dreams of barbaric imagination can surpass the fantastic creations of the civilized world; the idolatry of wood and stone and dead men's bones; the canonized impostures which a land, the foremost in the revival of letters and arts, has contrived to draw from the pure fountain of the Gospel. Startling to reason as they are, all these corruptions of religion may be traced to a common origin in human nature. Nor will this conclusion want abundant confirmation in any branch of human science; whether fire, or generative nature, or earth, or heavenly bodies were adored by the Persian or Chaldean sage of old time, or public opinion is to be enthroned in the seat of Providence by a modern German wizard.*

You may trace these fantastic varieties into the capricious workings of a few common and notorious elements, severally determined by the local and political or social circumstances of their production and development. All, however, when broadly surveyed with respect to the whole of human progress and its true laws of change, will not obscurely suggest some common source—some original idea, quite beyond the range of mere untaught barbarism—a primitive worship, communicated with the first essential instruction—but, in the course of generations, subject to those causes of change and corruption which are still seen working on every human institution, but, most of all, on religion—a result for which we might borrow a passage from the Christian apostle: "Because that when *they knew God*, they glorified Him not as God, neither were thankful; but became vain in their imaginations, and their foolish heart was darkened. Professing themselves to be wise, they became fools." They became philosophers; they discovered Braminical and Budhist doctrines of ideas, and the profound fact of the unreality of things—they untied the bonds of creation, and dissolved the causal order of nature. They discovered the sage doctrine of Pantheism, and found divinity in the elements. "They changed the

---

* Hegel.

glory of God, the uncorruptible God, into an image made with hands like unto corruptible man, and to birds, and four-footed beasts, and creeping things," &c. Such was the earlier stage of a process which has never ceased, however it may have changed its outward form from brutal ignorance to artful priestcraft, or to depraved passions, avarice, ambition, and unhallowed lusts, or to idle speculations : in whatever fashion creature worship or demon worship has originated, from the realms of Mokanna or Budha to the chair of Gregory the Great. There is no mystery in the history of superstition, when one elementary fact is taken first : the same obscuring vapor, from the crucible of the same old alchemist, may have sent up the same fantastic sublimations—false gods and lying oracles and subtle speculations, to overlay, and, if possible, to exclude the one original truth. Thus, according to this view of the actual course of the one element of social progress, that can be immemorially traced—some one original communication, or instituted ordinance must have afforded the material for the countless aberrations of human worship and doctrinal error. As all civilization has been very clearly shewn to have resulted from some original instruction ; so all religion may be inferred to have originated in some one simple, pure, single form, communicated at the first, to supply the first elements of control and moral guidance, when no other can have existed ; and to afford the indispensible conditions of early civilization.* For this conclusion,

---

* Note A. and Whately's Lectures on Political Economy, chap. 5.

it may fairly be asked that some distinguishable traces should be found. Such there are, indeed, as many and as strong as any reasonable scepticism can demand. I cannot here enter in detail on the vast sea of ancient mythology, happily explored by many able antiquarian writers and commentators, Maurice, Bryant, Jones, and many who have successfully availed themselves of their researches, or followed in their tracks. So elaborate a review is, indeed, as needless as it would be unsuitable to the limited compass of this inquiry. There is enough notorious to all educated minds, of the facts to which I shall but briefly refer, as undisputed ground for the inference which may be thus briefly stated.

If all, or most of the creeds of heathen antiquity, were severally to be stripped of such tenets and traditions as *are not common to all*—or, are traceable to some local origin, there would be found to remain a few original elements of great refinement and power, resulting from no philosophy, nor bearing any character of human invention, yet found in the most remotely separated nations, languages, and religions, manifestly offering a nucleus to all. On these, philosophical theism may (as it often has done), construct subtle theories, and assign to aboriginal man reasons impossible to the untaught, and little agreed in by the learned; but such are only to be rationally explained as the surviving and indestructible elements of an original religion.

In these we should expect to discern the probable indication of the first communicated religion; and they should be found in some form of combination in any claiming to be so considered. The creation, by the Ruler and Disposer of all things, of man and the world he inhabits; the worship of one God, the Maker of heaven and earth; the institution of sacrifice; the fall of man; the existence of an evil Power at enmity with God; the promise of some divine restorer; the mysterious notion of the Trinity, beyond the range of conception: such are among the residuary elements so variously disguised in many forms among numerous local superstitions. With these, are facts of tradition or historical record, which similarly obtain a common consent in the memory of different races. And the question is reduced to this; in what religion and record they can be found to be combined in one simply consistent and homogeneous structure? Such a combination of the common, and apparently prime elements, carries all the evidence that probable reasoning can afford or require. But there is with this, a very important feature of the case, to be observed in the essential character of these elementary doctrines, as compared with the mass of heathen accretions. For while these latter bear the manifest evidence of human invention, the former are, on the contrary, wholly irreconcilable with such a source; they are beyond the grasp of the most enlightened reason of modern times; they cannot be deduced from any transformation of heathen superstitions; while it is as easy to see how all heathenism can be framed out of distorted conceptions of these high original elements.

Upon the strictest research, if such in so plain a matter can be required; by (I may say) the common consent of all history and all questionable tradition, there can be found but one creed or policy to satisfy any of the conditions of this inquiry. Within that collection of ancient volumes, which is received by the civilized world as sacred, under the term of Holy Scriptures; and authenticated so far as the evidence of authenticity can be applied to ancient records; received as containing in its compass the oldest writings of which there is any account; we have, first, one continued series of events and progressive changes for upwards of fifteen centuries, down to our own historic era; next, a progress strictly continued for eighteen centuries further, down to the times in which we live. This far-grasping history is further extended back to the origin of the human race, by an authoritative statement of the genealogy of the fathers of the Jewish race, composed when the traditions of family ancestry and the main changes and determining events could not fail to be in remembrance, and preserved by records and monuments. And I here observe that, though we have no probable trace of the existence of alphabetic writing before the time of Moses,* still of picture writing there are numerous and undoubted remains, going back beyond any ascertained date. Nor are we certain that there did not exist a rude form of syllabic writing, of which there are many remains, to which it would be hard to assign a date.

The continuity essential to a main and final purpose of the Creator, is thus strongly indicated in the religion and history of the Bible. For this important claim we are in no way dependent on mere historic testimony; for

* Note A.

without referring to its intrinsic character (already described) of originality, it contains in itself other indications far more sure. The mere fact that it stands alone in any rationally admissible claim to either originality or continuity, may seem to be enough to establish its place; and the first of these qualifications must tend to confirm the other. Its continuity would thus be presumable through periods of which there is no historic trace. And, though not depending on this mode of inference, I must observe that it very much goes to confirm the inferences derivable from more specific data.

In groping amid monuments and traditions, the historian of antiquity is liable to be led astray by narrow and partial indications, by local traditions, and by the attractions of theory. The clouds in the distance take form and local habitation, and give ample work to the ruthless hand of the historical sceptic who may follow on the enthusiast's track of discovery. But, as we approach the dim confines of tradition, where little can be ascertained on satisfactory evidence, we must, so far as the quest can be considered reasonable, proceed on broader grounds. And it may be regarded as the high claim of the single case now under inquiry, that it is the only one which can, with reasonable certainty, afford clear indications of reality beyond this doubtful line.

This confirmation arises from the *systematic connection* between all its facts, and the *systematic completeness* of all its proofs, records, monuments, and moral adaptations. It will thus be found to stand upon a broad analogy, which advances to a certainty not inferior to demonstration, as its compass of proof expands. Let me explain this law of reason : of which the case of religion is the most complete instance and illustration. In every question of probable evidence, the assurance grows in an accelerative ratio with the increasing combination of facts; for every added fact must tend to limit the number of possible solutions, and (what more especially bears on this inquiry) as the accumulation advances, every separate fact becomes more exclusive in its application. Thus, also, it seems evident that less ascertainable facts, essential to the conclusion so determined, become probable on the force of the connected whole. Thus, for example, when we contemplate the unquestionable evidences which fix the genuineness and authenticity of the Scriptural records of events from the era of Moses, or the period then within the memory of man, up to the day of the evangelists, any statement contained within that line of narration, which might seem open to question, must still in reason be understood to be true, in some way wholly consistent with the system of authentic facts. And thus, also, the mere continuity of a series of events bearing one single purport implied throughout, offers the strongest proof of the reality both of the whole and of its proposed design.

We do not here insist that every statement in such a historic line of records is to be necessarily understood, or even reconciled to human notions, as may perhaps be demanded in a narrative of events merely human. Recollecting that we speak of a Divine agency governing events to an end yet unknown, we are not in a condition to judge what may be expedient, according to this purpose ; or what, in the long course of a remote line of administration, even the progress of the temporal conduct of the plan may require, or have required. But we can confidently pronounce, as a rational conclusion, that *some* necessary connection must exist between the obscure or mysterious fact and the ascertained system; or that the statement which we may fail to understand is explicable by perfect knowledge, in some way essentially just and true; that the unknown cannot be other than what the known requires. Such is the law of reason, recognized by all sound philosophy in every other branch of knowledge, though so often forgotten when it might be most conclusively applied. In this special case, this application has a completeness not otherwise to be found: it has that highest evidence which belongs to a system, and affixes a limit to objections and rash theories framed on the ground of what cannot be understood, or what does not appear.

The records of the Old Testament offer all the characters of a system beginning far back in remote periods of duration, involving conditions antecedent to the world's time, and including results beyond it, implying all within these limits to be but portions of a larger whole. Hence any theory, whether moral or spiritual, which omits the distinct observance of this great main fact, is (so far as it is not pernicious error) merely frivolous. In a case in which every incident must be properly understood to have some relation to provisions for an unknown result, the inquiry must be prosecuted, not in the solution of what seems doubtful, nor in that which affords ground for varied or controverted theory, but in facts capable of the clearest proof, or upon those Divine declarations which are the most simple and direct. The facts, so far as they are authentic—the doctrines, so far as they come directly and unambiguously—the purpose, so far as it is to be clearly known—however short may be the light thus afforded—offers a sure and safe ground for the deductions of reason; to be yet more cautiously followed in proportion as the object is more remote and vast. There is a remark of Coplestone's as strikingly applicable as it is elegant in the style of expression. The bishop's observations relate to the use of terms and a wholly different topic, but will be easily seen to apply to that before us. " While we confine our attention to the ordinary occurrences of life, or to those relations of things with which we are familiar, no such precision or refinement is required; the commonest tools need not be made with mathematical exactness. But when we push our inquiries beyond this daily sphere of vision, greater and greater accuracy is required in the instruments we employ. The slightest impurities in the atmosphere, a floating atom, or the vibration of a footstep, will interfere with the observations of physical science, and throw us, perhaps, at once out of our course,

> 'Ten thousand leagues awry
> Into the devious air.' "

But the utmost precision of the instruments of human reason can be of no avail to gauge those infinite depths, in which all we know of the Divine determinations and of the recorded dispensations of God must probably have their yet unconceived results. It is easy to see what *is;* but when the intent is to be surmised, or when what is wanting, superfluous, or inconsistent, is to be pronounced, we are far less provided for the argument than if we were to undertake a theory of the universe, or a measure of the infinite.

When, however, all that we can with certainty observe is carefully compared, we can find in a small but far extended range of undoubted facts, the same kind of evidence which the harmonious arrangements of the solar system, and still nearer provisions of the globe we inhabit, offer, of an intent and a Power existing beyond the sceptic's wisdom to measure or scrutinize. I have already on a different occasion,* invited your attention to a special, and I believe, sufficient example of this evidence, and of the conclusions to which it leads. A long succession of events—of judgments—ritual ordinances, and circumstantial interpositions, appear in the gradual formation and growth of the Jewish dispensation; all having a visible connection with a remote unknown result, for which their tendency, unlike that of the universal occurrence of human and national progress, is exclusively explicable by the actual event. Like a vessel sailing against wind, and current, and tide, advancing in opposition to every law of human conduct, offering unless on the one assumption (denied by the sceptic), no ground of policy, no motive to human will, no clue to the far-off intent; and yet, when retrospectively seen down the range of generations, combined so as to manifest a pervading policy governing throughout. The rationalist will answer, that every event of time must be

---

* First Act Sermon, and Note B.

the result of all the preceding incidents out of which it may have arisen. But the objection does not apply; the case is wholly distinct. The Jewish history is not the mere narrative of a normal course of incidents, following according to the common laws of occurrence. It is a close series of acts of policy, all contrary to this law, all express, mostly without any of the usual motives of policy,—if referred to human aims, without meaning—in clear opposition to human interests—often impossible, unless by some higher control—unavailing, unless by virtue of some incident not to be foreseen, or rationally expected. Such,—confining ourselves to what ranks as authentic, on ordinary ground of historic record,—is the nature of the Jewish history from a period fully sufficient for a far stronger inference than we here are bound to arrive at. It may commence with the call of Abram, and be followed on through the succeeding carefully registered generations; the bondage; the wandering in the desert; the conquest of Canaan; the Levitical law; the theocratic policy, so wholly exclusive of all human aims and human wisdom; the long series of prophetic announcements well authenticated as to their period, yet so concealed as to their sense, till made clear by remote fulfilment. And finally—the result connecting all the past with all the future—summed in the beginning of a new dispensation, itself adapted to other times and exigencies still unknown. In this long line there becomes visible an unbroken chain and the plain footsteps of a single Power—a line to be dimly traced back to the promise in the fatal garden, and forward to the hour in Gethsemane.

Thus, amid the lapse of earthly things, one unbroken chain of connected dealing is to be traced. While empires and dominant races, creeds and philosophies, have in the courses of change driven each other down into oblivion, this one only offers the explanation of this visible system of things, or the traces of a design reconcilable with the creation of a being like man, or with the known character of the Creator. Detach your mental vision from local history and the specialties of time, and look broadly on the past of human progress; till its main characteristic features become perceptible, and you will, not indistinctly, discern the same one long series of connected dispensations, inseparably woven into every period of human advance, either directly or by remote influence. And when human records fail or become obscure, throwing upon them the only reliable light; still advancing with the advances of civilization, without a single breach of its continuity, changing its adaptations in conformity with human progress; and this by no capricious development from social causes, but by express and manifest interpositions, preconceived in its own system, predicted independently of social influences and in opposition to earthly policies and powers. On the other hand, it cannot fail to be remembered that all other forms of religion, or natural power, or civil institution, have been bounded and transitory, and have indicated no pervading or systematic connexion with the course of things.

There is—not to be omitted in this statement—one fact of great importance to this argument, but too plain and authentic to be carried beyond the bare affirmation.

The unity of this whole system is confirmed by the pervading continuity of not merely a chain of dispensations, but by one main principle so clearly preserved throughout. The fall of man and his restoration by a promised Redeemer are implied or expressed through all, and while these main elements seem to shew, by their universal diffusion, the depth of root from which they have so widely diverged; in this one standard form, they have the consistency and purity from admixture, and the main central place, which indicate the source. From the first announcement of the woman's seed in the garden of Eden, to the closing statement which explains it, the one thread runs through all changes and dispensations. Nor, in the present statement, is it to be omitted, that this connection is not simply to be traced by any mere analysis of the varied and sometimes obscure records of prophetic or poetical language. There is through every one of those dispensations an explicit recognition of all the former. First mystically announced at a period when there could have been no adequate language, or clue of experience, the promise was conveyed by type and symbol, or in the wrapping of figurative expression: as time went on, and as occasion called for nearer views of a consoling and encouraging promise, it received increased distinctness; still never fully understood until its accomplishment was effected by the very blindness of a race, not chosen for its wisdom or virtue, but to preserve the promise and be the instrument of its fulfilment. It was then, as St. John has written, and as might still without much qualification be written of later and wiser times, "the light shineth in darkness, and the darkness comprehendeth it not ;" to the accomplishment, the will of man contributed opposition only.

Assuredly, if we are to assume that the Author of this complex scheme of human existence has any purpose,— has not in vain so gifted and so endowed the dominant race to whom His earth is a possession, we must look for that purpose in the only indication which bears the character of a permanent institution,—the only presumable claims to a divine source,—the only civilizing and regenerating element of social amelioration, and the only grounded provision for man's future.

And, lastly, calling to mind all the better, higher, and purer elements of man's nature, so little called forth, so little satisfied in this world's life, in what earthly state or sphere is their use to be found if no further scope is designed? But where is that bright consummation of the Creator's design to be sought in sin and sorrow among departing things? Is there any religion or earthly polity not a mockery of human hope, until we come to the same time-rooted, divinely-revealed, and authenicated religion of promise which gives assurance of a hope not of earth?

If the foregoing considerations were all, they would be found enough for our inquiry, but they fall far short of all. It may be asked does our chain of continuity stop within the covers of the Bible? It would be impossible, within the narrow scope which I can here occupy, to open the wide field of subsequent confirmation. I shall have but time for the mere suggestion of two main topics.

The same extraordinary people, whom we have seen

so distinguished by Divine interposition, still subsists, fulfilling the destiny marked out for it expressly,—having, even by its crime, unconsciously fulfilled the purpose of its election, it yet continues to fulfil its doom of 3,000 years—an astonishment, a "proverb", and a "byeword" among all nations in which for many ages it has found "no rest for the sole of its foot"—still surviving to witness to nations the constancy of the Divine purpose, and hold to all who are not blind, the light it cannot itself see. In desolation, maintaining an unnatural separation, as if its atoms could not combine with the common elements of human nature. Here, in the light of recent experience, is another discernible chain which binds the present with the past. Unchanged in the nature once impressed by a superhuman system of discipline, they stand before the world's eye to attest the character and workings of that system—and to challenge and partly guide speculation for the future. I am indeed convinced, that if this people, fulfilling the common law of races, had been either cut off, or wholly absorbed into other nations, we should have profound theories to show that no such race could ever have existed.

But is this all? Has that Supreme Providence, which so long never left itself without witness—never lost sight of its purpose—been content, from that awful hour which fulfilled so many prophecies and summed such a course of things—at last committed the eternal purpose to the mere current of worldly change, and the natural progress of events? Omitting the obvious consideration, that all things must be supposed to work together towards the same predestined end, to which all the elements of the world are, in a measure, causal; a very simple and practical view of existing facts will sufficiently meet the question. If I were to ask of any one who now listens, in what race of men, in what language, and by what human agency those sacred memorials, and those doctrinal declarations, and sacred institutions have been most uncorruptedly preserved, adhered to, and propagated freely to every land under heaven; does not every heart inly echo the one favoured country's name—the land of freedom, of civil order and constitutional law, of commercial prosperity, of sober and tempered civilization, combining in its frame and spirit the influences of every just principle and true morality,—all founded upon the teaching of the one unadulterated rule of faith? Does not the missionary from the British Isles—does not the English tongue, now advancing with human progress over the globe of earth—most consistently fulfil the Apostolic mission? Does not every wind God breathes to waft the sails of the Christian island, carry tidings of great joy to millions who sit in darkness?

I have not thought it needful to pause upon a great fact, too plain for comment before this learned assembly, and suggestive of too many considerations not within my present aim—the broad but clear distinction between barbarism and civilization, precisely co-extensive with heathenism and Christianity: and not only so, but offering a graduated view of the several proportions in which each has been the instrument of moral and civil advance. I cannot now follow the gradations of European civilization and religion, or enter on the controversial topic which such a comparison should open; but I may safely revert to the land, from which, as a chosen centre, Providence appears to direct its main operations. It will not be held as a rhetorical exaggeration if I say that the English tongue will, in the retrospect of a distant future, obtain the character of a sacred tongue. When much that we call history shall be out of memory, and all that is the philosophy of the hour shall be buried in the same dust with the wisdom of the Egyptians, and covered with the spiders' pall, that language will spread, as it is spreading over half the habitable globe, and bear with it all that deserves to live of the laws and the letters of a chosen race—chosen, as were the Jews of old, not for their merits, but for the purpose they are destined to fulfil, happy, if they will but know and fully recognize their noble privilege—to whom in these latter days " have been committed the oracles of God."

It has been explained by ecclesiastical historians how, when the Old Testament dispensation had come to its end, the world was prepared by a remarkable concurrence of events, so as to prepare a more enlarged area, and a highway among the nations, for the next great advance which was to follow. Many a man who now speculates on the course of human events, and employs much political acuteness on the fortunes of peoples and governments, may not, in the complex movement of the elements of change, in the strife of national interests and ruling aims, apprehend the calm pervading advance of those influences which still, as of old, are conducting all things to their appointed end.

The distinction between those common, moral, and civil elements of social advance, which are in ordinary operation, and those unforeseen and seemingly accidental incidents, which from time to time come singly, and give new directions to the course of events, and accelerate the progress of nations, is most important to be here understood. For, while we must ascribe all the working elements of humanity to the same designing Power which has ordained the entire mechanism of life; yet it is in the latter we must look for the essential interposition of a guiding control. Thus, at the present day, a vast and wonderful concurrence of seemingly brilliant accidents, and of minds of the first order, have come together, in a single generation, to astonish the age, and wholly change the form and constitution of civilized society,—at a period when a great advance of religious effort, zeal, Christian liberality, and ministerial talent and learning, seem prepared to enforce and spread the cause of salvation. Once again, as in the Apostolic era, but in a manner, and by instrumentalities wholly beyond human foresight, or policy, the ends of earth have been brought together by railway, steamer, and telegraph, means providentially ordered in the appointed time; not to effect any material amelioration of merely social morals, to abate the play of the passions, or the stormy spirit of worldly pursuit; but simply to prepare, once again, the "highway" for the message of a loftier aim. I may recal to many here a very curious instance of an inadvertent application of the language of prophecy, by Laplace, under the notion that he was only describing the present age, by an apt quotation from Lord Bacon, at the head of his chapter on the History of Astronomy, in the *Systeme du Monde*. When the illustrious *savant* penned these words—

"*Multi pertransibunt, et augebitur scientia*"—had this great mathematician, who unhappily lived in an evil generation, and a land of spiritual darkness—had he any friend near to tell that this apt description of a coming period, thus applied and confirmed, by his own sagacious apprehension, was the prediction of an ancient prophet of Israel,—he, who was not inclined to look for truth in Scripture, would have managed to express it in other words. They, however, who have not rejected the witness of the oracles of God, may accept of this *unbiassed* testimony; this hostile acceptance of language which may be taken as the motto of the nineteenth century, and was intended to describe the approach of a new and final dispensation—" Many shall run to and fro, and knowledge shall abound." The social world is beginning to be shaken together; the low is made high, and the lofty levelled; the very wars which carry dismay and sorrow in their course, and overshadow the homes of every land, will tend to cast down the barriers between nations. When the dust and smoke of conflict shall have sunk, and the stain of slaughter be dried from the earth, a new level will appear, not for the competitions of commercial wealth, or for the increase of social acquisition, or the objects of popular striving, or anything in the common aims and tendencies of earthly wisdom. All these have arrived at their utmost. Humanity has reached its climacteric, and is already on the decline. It is then that a new order of events may be looked for; that it will be seen that the vast acceleration of every cause of change has not been to no end, more than in former times; that the Providence which rules all events for the end, has not been idle ; and that the concurrent growth of spiritual zeal, ability, and success, as signal as the contemporaneous triumphs of art, is but the beginning and precursor of a more final change.

If the perfectibility of mortal man, or the completion, in the sense of the socialist, of his earthly state, were a possible result, without some further provision far more efficient than any advance in knowledge, it would be no hard task to shew that all the requisite instruction is to be found in the ordinances, discipline, and precepts of the Christian religion, and there only. This, among other such facts not to be denied, may stand as an added indication of its claim; it is the very source of the whole moral order of civilized nations, and even of all that tends to moral advance in the heathenism of the more civilized heathens, who have at different periods drawn from the same fountain.

And when it is justly considered how practically opposed is its influence to the spirit of the world, so that even while its beauty and excellence have ever been frankly acknowledged, and its truth admitted by the reason, its moral teaching is evaded, its doctrines corrupted, and its facts *practically* disbelieved by the multitude, and this on no explicit grounds of reason: it may be felt that no power less than divine could have upheld and carried it down through all time—through the countless obstacles, amidst the wreck of empires, faiths, and philosophies,—to hold the high place it possesses in an age equally remarkable for its intellectual development and its sceptical tendencies ; but no less so for the expansive energy of its missionary spirit.

It would here be strictly in place, to observe upon the exclusive claim, of this one central source of all religion and order, to the moral system from which its secular influences are partly derived. The topic is extensive enough to demand separate notice in a future discourse. The moral precepts of the Gospel have now for a long time become a part of popular opinion, and (without the sanctions, or spiritual aid, from which their efficacy is derived), are, in various degrees, adopted in every creed and every ruling institution ; and still, when we seek to trace to any source but the one, these, seemingly, natural truths, on strict inspection, they appear to become more inscrutable in theory, and to be entirely beyond the scope of ethical philosophy. The peasant may repeat the rule, but the philosopher stumbles at the reason ; for the elementary theory of moral truth, virtue, and right, of rules of conduct which seem intuitive to the vulgar, and which rule every affection of the wise, you may grope through volumes of subtle, but conflicting speculation. A few precepts, claiming a divine origin, theoretically and practically include the wisdom of the wisest and the virtue of the best, pure and free from the corruptions of many ages and schools of philosophy. And while the pride of reason stumbles, the child can come to the fountain of truth. While the profound Theist may be both vicious and wretched, the sincere and whole-hearted believer may sit in light and peace, in the darkness and trial which are the lot the world gives to its worshippers. The over-burthened heart may lay down its load at the foot of the cross, and find the truth never taught by philosophy, though often sought—" Peace I leave with you, my peace I give unto you; *not as the world giveth* give I unto you."

In fine, Christianity alone is suited to the Present, as it was to the Past; and alone opens a future to the faith of man. This future is not *merely* to be inferred from a promise; Christianity also offers all the characteristic indications of adaptation to such an end. For this, its provisions are as plain as are the lessons of a school for the demands of commercial life. Every other institution or science has been the slow and long accumulating result of many ages and many minds; Christianity came in its perfect form from One, of whom his wondering and credulous contemporary asked, " Is not this the carpenter's son ?"—a great fact, which will not lose its power when you go on to find in that One the power, wisdom, and goodness which even the atheist and scoffer have allowed to be superhuman.

A religion from the Creator must necessarily, in every dispensation, possess two claims, without which it can have no pretension to acceptance on any just ground of belief. It must be offered on the express authority of Divine declaration, and this authority must be authenticated, agreeably to those practical laws of reason which belong to the intellectual nature of man. That is, the reason which governs the whole commerce of the present life. Now, in this argument, it is enough to allege, what will not be contradicted, that such are the precise grounds on which the Bible is believed by civilized nations as true, and by Christians as their ground of faith; and, further, in this respect it stands alone.

Among the essential distinctions between the Christian

and other religions, is the peculiar confinement of its doctrines and institutions to its expressed spiritual intent. It does not lay the foundation of any merely temporal scheme of dominion. And while its essential end is provided for both in doctrine and moral precept, it holds apart from such institutional ordinances and social interests as by their nature, and that of social progress, could not at the time be unchangeably fixed. Other religions have mainly respected either the interests of the priest and potentate, or, at best, the existing state of a country or a race. Christianity, in its very omissions, contains the condition of perpetual conformity. Carrying in itself the principle of civilization, it is accommodated to all its stages; and while unchangeable in doctrine and the elements of faith and worship, it leaves room for a Church polity and for the accommodation of all that is simply formal or administrative to the wants of the age and the general state of social institutions.

I have, so far, shewn that, on the conditions previously stated as the ground of such an inference, Christianity alone offers the essential indications of a connection with the final purpose of man's creation. I might securely rest in this conclusion; but it is, after all, but a part of the whole argument, which must be considered incomplete without some inquiry into the special provisions of the Christian scheme. To make this more satisfactory, I purpose first to take a brief survey of the condition of the human race, as it is represented in the statements of Scripture, and its actual agreement with this representation. We shall then be in condition to look more closely on the chief moral and doctrinal adaptations of the Gospel.

PART II.

MORAL AND DOCTRINAL ADAPTATIONS.

LECTURE IV.

ROM. III. 23.

"For all have sinned and come short of the glory of God."

I HAVE now arrived at the conclusion, that there is but one existing system of arrangements and provisions pervading the entire of human history from its remotest period, which appears to satisfy the conditions from which we have set out; that is, the existence of the Creator, of a purpose in His work, of adaptations for that purpose, and of the application of these considerations, in the highest degree, to man; and that, lastly, this one system, so described, is to be found in that religion of which the Bible contains the history.

I am next to apply this method of examination to such of the doctrinal and moral provisions of that religion as may be considered to be the main and fundamental elements of its creed; to see how far may be discovered their adaptation to the state of man as known, and to the spiritual design as revealed.

If we simply take our stand on the conditions and first conclusions of the former part of this argument, it might seem to be the inference that the original plan of the Creator should be expected to be carried out in its whole extent. And an apparent objection might arise, that such does not appear to be the actual case. The actual state of man, comprehensively surveyed, indicates many tendencies, seemingly inconsistent with such a conclusion. From this the sceptical inference, which has often been pressed, is that a plan so encumbered by failure cannot be ascribed to a Being possessed of infinite power. I shall, in the course of these lectures, have occasion to expose the fallacy and presumption of such objections. There is a special answer to the fallacy as now stated, as it is clearly to be shewn, that the present state of man cannot, on *any* assumption, be rationally viewed as a fulfilment of the original plan of his Creator; and further, that in the whole scheme of the religion of which we have stated the claim, this present state is recognized as evil, and met by provisions wholly remedial and antagonistic. But, independently of all authority, mere observation and experience will be enough to establish, that the existing state of the human race cannot be reconciled with the essential conditions of any original plan of the Creator, and must necessarily be concluded to be a *departure* from the first intent and divine conception of his being; after which we shall the better see what ought to be the statement and what the adaptations of religion, in respect of such a result.

Before entering on this exposition, I must guard against a false inference from the foregoing remark. It cannot be allowed that this departure indicates any defect in the first design. There was in man's creation every provision for a different result—instruction, law, natural intelligence, right and good affections, hope, fear, love, and the knowledge of the Creator. And if it may be said that the possibility of evil might have been excluded, I must reserve my answer for a further stage of this argument, and only now observe, that such an exclusion may have been inconsistent with the whole design, of which human life and man's world are but a little part. Nor is it conceivable, how such a barrier against moral evil could be ordained, but by the exclusion of moral freedom, and all the higher attributes of humanity. But waiving for the present a question so little within the scope of our reason, let us come to our proper ground.

Independently, as I have said, of all precedent and authority, it is almost, on the mere statement, a plain matter of observation, that the state of man is abnormal, a state of disorder, a plain departure from the law of his being.

The normal conditions of this life are plain enough for our present purpose; they are, with sufficient approximation, contained in every moral theory involving the rudest approaches to civilization—wherever rules of justice, honor, virtues, charity, have been recognized—wherever the social virtues and social interests have been acknowledged, or crime and social evil met the prohibition or penalty of law—whether we refer to the social philosophy of nations, or the elementary indications of the Divine intent already mentioned, or to the religious tenets of the civilized world—the normal law, the conditions of social and individual well-being are plain: but not less plain are the proofs of the moral and social frustration. Socially, morally, intellectually, in the individual or aggregate, man, evidently designed and framed for a state of law and order, stands nearly alone in the visible creation, as conformable to no steady order—the defier and despiser of rules and acknowledged ordinances—the breaker of his own laws, whether of prudence, of governing authority human or divine, or of personal concern. Separated from the brute of field and forest, scarcely more by superior gifts of intellectual power, than by the fatal privilege of lawless depravity.

This broad statement, unqualified as it may seem, may be submitted as an appeal to the recognition of universal experience, of which history, even to the remotest tradition, is the unbroken evidence, and every human monument a record. We might amass a rich compilation of human degeneracies, superstitions, monstrous perversions of power, intelligence, and Divine instruction; of wars and revolutionary massacres, lawless tyrannies, and abject slaveries, or, in a word, the constant ebb and flow of all human progress. We might also refer to the common self-conviction of human opinion, in which no man of ordinary intelligence is satisfied with himself or with his condition.

It is not here argued that, even in the elementary constitution of the human world, there is still wanting some main element, essential to complete the moral and social plan, and secure it from disorder and periodical collapse. Some such want may be, but it is not to be assumed. In man's moral constitution, in the fundamental principles and working processes of the social state, all the main conservative elements are, potentially, to be found. Virtue is known as virtue, justice as justice; the moral and social theories are in no way intrinsically defective so far as the concerns of life and workings of the social system require. Wrongs and crimes and follies have their suitable names. Nor can it be truly affirmed that the passions and sentiments to which all moral evil may be traced, were not originally provided for other good and useful ends, wholly different: there exists no *normal* law of evil from which it might be inferred to be part of the original conception or plan, or concluded that man, like the tiger or the shark, is what he was made to be. Yet so it is; evil is the characteristic result; the world is branded with a stamp not that of its Author. In the Divine Theocracy man is a rebel, adoring, trembling, and *resisting*. In the greatest empires the world has known, erected on the most specious policy and loftiest principles of patriotism and virtue, we find the result in the most consummate portraiture of human depravity—the Senate more base and degraded than the tyrants desire—the Cæsars succeeded by the Popes. I need not follow out these examples; it would be a summary of universal history. How startling, could we view it truly, is the moral picture of a world in which the purest principles of order and human welfare are ever acknowledged and trampled upon; in which the highest elevation and the loftiest praise—all glory, honour, and civil pre-eminence —are the reward of deeds of blood and devastation.

* * * "What do these worthies
But rob and spoil, burn, slaughter, and enslave
Peaceable nations, neighbouring or remote,

> Made captive, yet deserving freedom more,
> Than those their conquerors, who leave behind
> Nothing but ruin wheresoe'er they rove,
> And all the flourishing works of peace destroy,
> Then swell with pride, and must be titled gods,—
> Great benefactors of mankind, deliverers—
> Worshipped with temples, priests, and sacrifice."

We need not go so far as the poet. We must admit the fatal necessity which confers the laurel and the claim of the victor; but this is itself the proof and illustration of our state.

But it will be quite consistent with the principle of this inquiry, and better answer its main end, to compare the Christian with his own professed creed. The objection that the question is thus begged, is but apparent, as we do not thus take for granted anything we have to prove. The Christian religion is the received moral law of the civilized world,—more purely and wholly by nations in proportion to the perfection of their civil constitution. In this respect its perfection is admitted by the deistical philosopher; and I need not remind you of the eulogium of Rousseau upon its Founder. But this comparison, while placing the present argument on its strongest ground, will enable us most readily to trace the recognition of sin in the system by which the Creator has thought fit to meet it. It is yet enough that the highest indication of the social order is in the precepts and provisions of the Christian creed. With this qualification I may avail myself of the apostle's clear, explicit language, in speaking of the world that, as in the days of old, knows God, yet honours him not as God! that assents to a rule of faith, hope, and charity, and is still in subjection to all the opposing influences. The multitude that walks on that "broad way" which its professed creed abjures and denounces; and that, in its entire conduct, tramples upon, spurns, and denies the profession it supposes itself to recognize and hold as sacred, as a rule of life and a charter of redemption; verifying thus the terrible invective of Jesus on the Scribe and Pharisee of old. Such, beyond denial, is the world that acknowledges the gospel and keeps a convenient religion of its own—which makes "provision for the flesh to fulfil the lusts thereof"—which looks without hope to a life beyond the grave, without fear to an everlasting woe—that has a smile of scorn for all earnestness that transgresses beyond its own limit of formality; and yet, would call down fire from heaven to vindicate a theory or a form. Thus, whatever may be the source or genuine authority of the gospel, we have a stupendous *self-contradiction*, unaccountable save on the admission of some disturbance of the original design. Thus, man's world has stamped on its surface, in broad characters, which those who run may read, the mark of a departure, not ascertainable elsewhere within the compass of nature. It is thus enough to look on the Christian community—the world in its state of least degradation—Christian in name, in profession, in moral theory, and in its recognition of fundamentals—assenting to facts, which, if sincerely received as realities, are such as to shake the strongest heart, or make all worldly objects worthless in comparison, yet, withal, not awakening any genuine sense conformable to such facts, or any true indication in the crowd, nor often in the individual, of any sincere belief. That the facts of revealed religion are received as unquestionable truth, I do not in the least doubt; nor should I feel it difficult to explain much of this enormous contradiction.* For the present, it is enough to call your attention to the actual reality; it is the main aspect of the world in respect to its faith. Displaying all the plain indications of unquestioning assent; no more doubting the truths of the New Testament, than it doubts the truths of an arithmetical treatise, or a volume of astronomy; and both adopting its formal institutions and showing all readiness to dispute about its doctrines, but all the while displaying remissness, and, even in its very conformities, an unconsciousness of the real import of these admissions. Not doubtfully exhibiting the aspect of remissness in its Sabbath garb, when it offers its cold, formal homage to Him, whom it spends six days of the seven in forgetting, and questionably recognizes then. Such is the religion of the world; and let it be remembered, that in so representing it, I say no more than Jesus and his apostle more strongly intimate. (Matt. vii. 13, Rom. viii., &c. &c.) Admitting all that can be claimed for the comparatively few who are not ashamed of the Gospel of Christ, I must be understood to speak of the world whose religion is a creed, and no more; whose faith is shut up in the formularies and articles, with which they are not practically acquainted. And my affirmation is, that in this point of view it offers the most prominent phase of self-contradiction, an incon-

---

* The moral and intellectual theory of unbelief may be found fully discussed in "Letters on the Philosophy of Unbelief."—Fellowes, London, 1835.

sistency between profession and practice, monstrous in the universal harmony of God's Creation; a charge made good, not against ignorance and folly, but against the wise of this world, and against human nature. Not the reproach of false theories, or barbarian superstitions, but of the Christian world with its creed; a creed approved by evidence commensurate with all the laws of credibility; with man's history; and unshaken by the powers of sceptical ingenuity. We are, it is true, too familiar with the outward aspect of the world, perhaps too much bound by its chain of habit, to realize very clearly such a state of things in its true character. We are walking in "a vain shadow," in which all beyond is imperfectly conceived. We are wrapped in the atmosphere of human life—

"The smoke and stir of this dim spot
   Called earth."

Let us for a moment try to obtain a distant view, to see this familiar scene in a remoter aspect. Suppose, if it is not too much to ask, some inhabitant of that holier world which the Christian's creed admits, where the angel is said to rejoice over the sinner's repentance, to come down, as in earlier times, to visit the scene of the great conflict with the serpent, and with a curious interest, which an angel might well be supposed to feel, to witness and estimate the results of that immortal victory upon the cross. Now, judging in the only way you can, by your own human feelings; what do you feel might be his expectation, and what his impression from the reality. On his first far approaches, you may suppose him recalling the main terrible and affecting events of that momentous history, and listening for some far echo of the universal hymn of grateful love and adoration. He might expect to hear the voice of nations, of races, and languages, swelling into hallowed harmony, like the rush of many rivers, toward the throne of God, to the mercy seat on high; and he would hasten with a solemn and awe-struck countenance to explore this world of ours; this ancient monumental globe on which the Son of God once stood in human form to suffer death for man. What might be the amount of such expectations is beyond poor human reason to grasp, but we can, perhaps, more easily conceive the rush of sterner and sadder feeling awakened on the nearer view—how unlike the lowest reasonable expectation would be the reality— to us too familiar to be startling. Bear with me, if I carry this illustration one step further. After a mournful survey of our Christian world, what might be his wonder to discover our possession of authentic records; of elaborate creeds and articles of doctrine; of costly institutions and consecrated fabrics; and that there exists among us no material or spiritual want of provision for worship. Now, in this seeming stretch of fancy, I have only endeavoured to represent the effect of an unprejudiced first-view of circumstances, too familiar to us to be as impressive as they should be: habitual darkness loses its character to the accustomed eye. To the multitude, there is wanting a clear apprehension of its own deviation; to the world, respecting as it does the outward aspect of religion, its religion is little more than formal observances and the business of priests and ecclesiastical commissioners. But enough; such is the world; a state of disorder, an abnormal branch of God's creation; and that, the main branch within our field of observation; a chasm in the harmonious chain of order. Now, this must be *recognized*; and in some degree explained and provided against in any religion of which the doctrines and facts have a claim to be counted true. These conditions are to be found satisfied in the history and doctrinal statements of the Bible only. In the ancient records of the Penteteuch, the fall of man is represented, and the only cause reconcileable to reason intimated; while next, throughout the whole of the sacred volumes, there runs the gradual development of a remedial system terminating in an institution, the most profound if regard be had to its philosophy; the most effective if we look to its practical machinery; and the most comprehensive if seen in relation to the nature of God and that of man—the present, past, and future—to the sin, the remedy, and the end.

To trace this in the special adaptations, the essential condition of our argument, we must recognize the state of man in its more latent *individual* working. Our statement, so far, reaches only to the affirmation and proof of a general fact. The secret infirmity of the human heart is little to be detected in the specious tone and language of the world. Both, are human nature, cause and effect to each other; each giving and receiving influences different in form, much the same in result; each differently disguised and differently expressed.

In the commerce and common intercourse of the world private passions are sunk, and general interests have developed laws of opinion and outward show, which tend, by constraining influence, to conceal what man is. The world, with all its vast amount of error, is wiser than its component atoms.

There exists an abundant repository of accumulated experience; a far descending development of rule, maxim, and impression, with a general freedom from private impulse; all of which confer an imposing front on that impersonal being which we call the public. Individual self-concealment helps to eliminate the vices from public morality; the individual contributes his formal assent to recognized rules of right and order: but the million such assents seem to express an amount of wisdom or goodness supposed to have some local abode.

In thus seeming to take a disparaging view of private virtue, I would not refuse due allowance for the worth of many individuals; still less would I be understood to question the sanctity of numerous eminent Christians. Such will be the last to object to a statement for which they have, besides experience, an authority they receive without demur. If such instances were not, the remedial scheme for which we enquire could not be verified; the sentence of utter inefficiency would render all proof idle—Satan would be the victor, the work of grace vain.

It is not, however, the open enemy, the doubter, still less the crotchetty rationalist, I propose to instance as the example of individual deviation—of the deep inconsistency which it is my present object to bring distinctly into view. Such are exceptional cases; instances, perhaps, of intellectual malformation; cases in the morbid anatomy of the human understanding; for (whether the

New Testament be true or false) such is the character hitherto belonging to every instance of sceptical philosophy. My present position is, the existence of the same abnormal character, the contradiction between conduct and *admission* in the individual as in the mass; and, to illustrate its extreme limit, it is the professing, rightly intending, justly asserting, orthodox Christian, I must call into court. Our present business is with him who fully assents to a creed of which he believes himself to have no doubt; who knows, so far as opinion can be called knowledge, where safety and where destruction lies, according to his creed; who knows that he must die, and believes that he is to be judged; who is weekly, perhaps daily, made aware that a great change of heart, a putting off the "old man," is required; who sees the narrow way and can warn others; yet moves on with the world, from day to day putting off the account—resolving and relapsing into forgetfulness—still carried back with the many, which (according to his belief), walk on the broad way "that leadeth to destruction."

Now such is the common description of the mass of nominal Christians, who "hold a form of godliness, denying the power thereof." If we look to State religion, we have ecclesiastical authority without spiritual respect; legislative recognition without faith; crowded churches without devotion; individual striving without consistency or progress; an admitted rule of faith, made plain as language can express; the facts simply stated and fully admitted; taught in childhood's earliest lessons; authenticated to reason in every mode and form that reason knows; not rendered doubtful by any effective objection; offering grounds for hope or fear far beyond any other conceivable object or result; and, to crown all, so entirely received by the common consent of opinion, that scepticism ever shrinks from the world's eye, and bears the strongest stamp of social disapproval. Such is the strongly ratified claim, and such the lax and ineffectual conformity,—such is the main condition which ought to be broadly and distinctly recognized and provided against by *special adaptations*. If we look for this recognition, or these adaptations in any other form of religion, or any scheme of moral rule but one, the search will be vain.

For, when we look to see in what scheme of polity, what philosophy or system of jurisprudence, there is to be found any express *recognition* of this great prevading condition, the main character of humanity inwardly and outwardly—in its aggregate and individual form—the search will be vain till we come to the apostle's demonstrative exposition of the "law of sin," generally affirmed in the fearful clauses of the first chapter of Romans, and individually brought home in the further statement of the same great argument, the most comprehensive statement ever brought into so brief a space. "I find then a law, which, when I would do good, evil is present with me—for I delight in the law of God after the inward man—but I see another law in my members, warring against the law of my mind, and bringing me into captivity to the law of sin, which is in my members."* Here in these few words is more of the true theory of human nature, than sage or sophist ever taught in porch, or grove, or academic chair. And

* Rom. vii. 21–23.

it leads to the fountain head of all earthly degeneracy, far beyond the comprehension of the present argument; the origin and centre of all the storms which from the beginning have swept over and laid waste in turn all the empires of earth, and every boasted structure of human power and policy. Here the theoretic goodness is reconciled with the practical infirmity; the formal reverence with the essential slight; the occasional excitement with the habitual oblivion; the fatal atrophy of the sad original disease, a "law of sin."

These facts are all notorious enough to impose some reluctance in any attempt to impress the consequence —were it not for the place they must take in this enquiry, and the weight of sceptical inference which they are often used to support. This fact is worth a moment's pause.

Go state this case of human inconsistency to the philosophic unbeliever, whose observing faculties are so often swallowed up by the abstractions or by the conventional fallacies on which his logical acuteness is wasted. He will inadvertently read you a severe lesson; he will assure you (an assurance I have often received) "If I believed half what you profess, how differently would I act; you say that you believe in such and such momentous facts. If this profession were sincere, you could not seem so much at your ease; these hopes and these objects of fear and awe do not admit of any other concern; if your theories and dogmas respecting the future were true, all earthly cares are frivolous; you are deceiving yourself with hollow conformities and idle professions." It is needless to offer the obvious answer to these fallacies—which, fallacious as they are, cast a severe censure on the natural inconsistency of human profession. They but reflect the dark aspect of fallen humanity, and illustrate the "law of sin," which brings "into captivity," the better reason and affections of the assenting, but, unconvinced professor, who "holds the truth in unrighteousness." We have thus a more elementary view of the great and universal disorder for which we are to look both for a distinct recognition, as well as for some remedial provision such as may be conformable with the purpose already inferred, and with the whole system of religion to which our reasoning has conducted.

If the foregoing statement be fairly understood, it describes a condition not confined to Christian lands or Christian profession; but it is curious to reflect that, prevalent as is the inconsistency of human reason and motives in all things, it appears most clearly and broadly in relation to that very system which, from its intent, is to be viewed as in direct antagonism with the present state of man.

This anomalous condition cannot by any effort of rightly directed reason, or in accordance with the actual analogy of what is known in nature, be reconciled with any supposable design of the Originator of all nature. The sum of things known is characteristically a scheme of order. The planet pursues its course according to the direction and velocity first imparted by the Almighty arm; the slow changes of land and sea follow their laws of change according to those natural forces and affinities by which the order of the world is maintained. Animal and vegetable nature have, throughout, their uniform adaptations to the whole system of life; all works together to promote the comfort, and the dominion, which is the original allotment of man. But man himself has revolted, as higher spirits are said to have rebelled. Human nature alone manifests a law of confusion, disorder, and self contradiction, a "law of sin." Man stands separate from the universal system, by the broad interval of vice, crime, improvidence, and the abuse of the highest gifts. When the traveller visits foreign lands, and stops to contemplate the sites of ancient empire, his wonder is awakened by the strange apparition of wide-spread and massive ruins, which, while they offer impressive illustration of the transitory nature of mortal achievement and human pride, bear at the same time witness to man's magnificence of design and high endowment. Not dissimilar is the lesson which we have thus to receive from this aspect of man; indicating, in the disordered elements of his existing state, the plain marks of a design unparalleled in its features of moral and intellectual beauty—in its potential provisions for happiness and virtue—for which, however ineffective, no provision is wanting. Manifesting the scattered lights, justice, virtue, love, gratitude, heaven-aspiring intellect; like the "garden-flower grown wild," choked with weeds over the fragments and the fallen pillars of a grand and glorious creation; and evidencing, at the same time, the magnificent plan and the sad frustration, and plainly speaking that it is not so it was first designed—that the hand of an adversary has been laid upon it. Well may we pronounce, upon the mere evidence of all we can learn of man's past, or see of his present state; "an enemy hath done this." And such, I need not here say, is the first record of the earliest tradition of man.

The case is now before us. Let us next see what modifications it must seem to claim in the remedial scheme, which should plainly—so far as reason may be applied to things far beyond its entire compass—be expected to meet such a state of deviation from a prime order, from the original conception of man's creation. This will better appear from a brief summary of the foregoing statement: man created for subjection to moral order and Divine law—endowed with suitable qualifications—and informed by appropriate instructions and discipline and Divine communication—departing wholly from his allegiance, and becoming in enmity with the ruling Power, and subject to a law of condemnation, the necessary result of Divine justice. Consequently unprovided with any extenuating plea, on the ground that he could offer nothing over and above his bounden obedience—but still continuing to stand out in rebellion, and departing more and more from the intent of his creation. Such is the first condition manifested in man—and affirmed by the earliest record of sacred history. Hence the necessity of some Divine provision independent of human virtue or obedience, yet so administered as concurrently to exact from man those essential elements of moral restoration. Hence the atonement.

Secondly,—The needful conformity thus required for the effectual application of this vicarious expedient, is found not sufficiently compatible with the disordered capacity of the human heart and mind; and, therefore, some provision must be looked for, in aid of man's infirmity. Hence spiritual aid and free grace.

Thirdly,—Some link of moral connection must be sought between the existing nature of man and the state to which he is to be restored; such as to purify the good from the evil of his state of being, and in some sufficient measure to approach the original conception of his origin. Hence the Gospel ethics.

These conditions, though very far below the entire comprehension of the whole design out of which they have their beginning and must have their end, are all, so far, clearly within the range of rational inference, which will find confirmation in the most unquestioned statements of Christian ordinance. At either limit, questions enough arise to be dealt with by dogmatic science. But so far, I submit, we have a complete view of what I shall describe as a scheme—part, doubtless, of a wider scheme, but still complete in its present adjustment to all we see and learn of man.

It involves the principle of the atonement and free grace; of justification by faith; of spiritual aid; and of the declaration of the moral law essential for the rectification of humanity. Of these provisions the adaptation is clear, so far as they are here in question; it is by no means requisite to the end of this inquiry, that we should explain or distinctly comprehend their essential fitness, or the elementary law of their operative effect—they offer the only adequate solution of man's state; and will, when separately contemplated, each offer some characters of manifest expediency to which I shall have occasion to advert in my remaining discourses. But at present I have only to observe, that is is not to be presumed that human reason within its proper limit—experience or direct revelation—can have the remotest apprehension of the undeclared counsels which may govern the administration of God's universal kingdom. The rudiments of eternal justice; the origin of law, fitness, expediency; what may be a necessity of the universal system, what not, are beyond reason; all things we know, but most especially those things which concern the kingdom of God, have their origin and end in another sphere of being. There are, it is true, presumptions, which by a cautious adherence to the analogy of God's known dealings, may supply some interesting confirmations fully adequate to sustain the course of inference proposed in these lectures—as I trust hereafter to show.

In conclusion, I have but to observe, that the actual phenomena of human disorder which constitute our case in this lecture, have all their correspondent affirmation and remedial adaptation in the statements and doctrinal provisions of the Bible and the Christian dispensation. The fall of man; the occasion and the author; the sentence; the numerous prophetic announcements, and moral as well as ritual laws; the uniform and prevading assertion of sin and enmity; of human inability and Divine grace, with the promise of spiritual aid. To this may be added the complete and perfect standard of moral conduct; in the New Testament, only, placed on its true ground of principle; and we have the outline of a system standing alone for both truth to experience and perfect adaptation to its declared and manifestly desiderated end, the restitution of immortal souls to a state which is the end of their first creation; and the only end antecedently probable from the consideration of their privileges, natural endowments, and Divine Author.

On the mysterious doctrine of the Trinity it must here be enough to say, that while it has in it no ground of antecedent improbability, it is clearly shadowed out in the conditions heretofore stated. They offer the several requisite agencies indicated in the creation, redemption, and spiritual recovery of man. In these operations there is not only a manifest necessity, but also a manifest distinction of character in the respective agencies. To say more would be to transgress the limits of sane argument. The doctrine is of God—and, taken on his own plain and direct authority, not to be anticipated or understood. Enough, we have by observation and experience the triple field of operation, the triple office, and the threefold aspect of Godhead; the unity and separate personality clearly expressed; a doctrinal fact, which reasoning can only obscure, but which the sobriety and sound common sense of the practical Christian will ever hold as a truth of God, to exalt and truly direct the piety, but above the reason, of man.

To an assembly of Christian teachers and students, acquainted with the Scriptures and practised in the rules of reasoning—it may be needless to insist farther on this remarkable concurrence between a state of facts so old and universal, and their very peculiar doctrinal statements, shewing a wide-grasping scheme of arrangements co-ordinate in origin and course of progress, and adapted with a discriminating exactness not to be explained by the philosophy of any age, but that derived from Christianity itself.

This concurrence of phenomena will, however, be much strengthened by a careful inspection of the moral theory of the Gospel, in which its immediate effect in relation alike to time and eternity will appear to no small extent, so far I have, in dwelling on the plain reality of observation and experience, but insufficiently amplified the comprehensive affirmation of the Apostle, " For all have sinned and come short of the glory of God ; being justified freely by His grace through the redemption that is in Christ Jesus."

LECTURE V.

1 Cor. xiii. 13.

"And now abideth faith, hope, and charity—these three; but the greatest of these is charity."

In any religion accordant with the conditions hitherto explained and understood in these lectures, and with the facts more particularly stated in the last, we are not only to look for a doctrinal system of suitable statements and provisions, consequent upon, or remedial for, the fallen state of man as alleged in the Scriptures and exemplified in the world; but there should also be looked for a reformatory system adapted for the intellect and affections of a free moral agent like man. His affections are to be purified and turned to their proper object; his intelligence is to be informed, and his course guided and prompted by motives adapted to his nature, and at the same time conformable to the main end. I have already affirmed the essential requisite of spiritual aid; but the capacities with which man is originally endowed for the Divine plan were to be also provided for and called in operation. His fallen nature was to be restored, his will and affections changed, and his course and conduct in life brought into conformity with that prime design—the moral and spiritual allegiance from which he has departed.

The conditions thus required may be subjected to a three-fold test; we may look for an adaptation to the intellectual principle which mainly governs the actions of man,—for an adaptation of spiritual motives,—and for the adaptation of a moral reformatory principle, in its two-fold bearing on the present and future.

Here, then, is a combination, very peculiar in its wholeness, and manifestly wanting in every known scheme of polity or religion but the one in which we have already found so many indications of Divine design. It is almost needless to add that, not only in Christian but in all partially civilized nations, there is a large infusion of Christian morals: but it is only at the source, where they exist in their originating elements, with their proper sanctions and unmixed with foreign elements, that they will be found to bear the Divine stamp, or to produce their perfect work.

In the language of the text which I have prefixed to this lecture, you have in three words brought together the moral system of Christianity—faith, hope, and charity. Like the day-beam, in which three original hues supply alike the light of day and all the various tints which ornament the face of nature, these three compose the light of the Christian heart.

It would seem enough to announce this happy combination, simple and seemingly obvious, though unconceived by human philosophy, to suggest the theory of a perfect state : but the motive and sanction would still be wanting in any temporal system ; so that it is not only adapted, but exclusively adapted to the Christian scheme.

Here there is an extraordinary test. On examination, it will appear that this combination includes all the moving elements of man's nature for good ; while it requires a complementary addition only to be found in the religion of the Gospel.

Faith realizes the objects of hope and love. Hope supplies and enlivens motives and affections. Charity is the bond of union with God and man; in no obscure sense "the fulfilling of the law," the intent of the "first and great commandment," and of the second, which "is like unto it." Take the apostle's definition in Corinthians,* and you cannot fail to apprehend that it singly contains the principle and all the conditions of a moral restitution of human nature.

It may be admitted that these elements must, already, from their self-evident uses and place in the moral scale, be variously involved in man's nature, and therefore included in some partial form, in the mass of ethical or religious systems. I claim no special allowance for the mere fact that faith, hope, and charity are presented as moral elements of Christianity: the distinction lies in this; they are its moral components, *neither more nor less*—the *integral* parts of a whole.

And if the systematic completeness of that whole be compared with the confused and partial combinations in all other ethical theories, it may be discerned that these three elements were only to be selected and combined from the vast maze of human motives and rules, by an eye cognisant of the inmost recesses of the heart, and for a design distinct from all the aims of human philosophy or legislative theory. Faith is, we may admit, an essential first principle in the commerce of life; hope a main

* xiii. 4—7.

motive; and the many virtues included in Christian charity are necessarily involved more or less in every ethical system : they are all main elements of man's nature latent in the whole texture of life. As a few simple material elements are involved in a thousand substances, undetected but by the highest art, so are these simple elementary motives extricated, and combined by the skill of the master mind, into a system alone adapted for His declared end; a combination which has been manifestly framed to combine with and form an essential and correlative portion of that higher doctrinal system referred to in my last discourse. This will more distinctly appear presently. But first let me offer a very few words more on the ethical theories of man.

When we enquire what human wisdom has of itself done to throw any theoretic light on the rules of conduct and the path of life, we cannot but be struck with the varying and conflicting speculations upon a subject of which the elementary facts are thought to be so plain to observation. It is needless now to speak of the sages of antiquity. The moral philosophy of later and more enlightened times has improved little on earlier foundations. In his usual endeavor to find heathen reasons for Christian obligations, the casuist has endeavored to construct his theories on grounds of principle not absolutely untrue, but partial, confused, and disjointed from the first principle. The light of nature, fitness, the beauty of virtue, or self-love, or universal benevolence, the moral sentiments, or the public good. I deny none of these prime elements of human conduct. A true theory of moral sentiment should include them all.

All that reason and experience can discover as grounds of conduct, and as expositions of actuating sentiment, may be assumed to enter into a correct view of the moral law. They are imperfect results from the natural affections of man created in the image of God; and are no obscure indications of his original and destination; but altogether insufficient for the restoration which that destination claims, and which is the express design of revealed religion.

In the ethical system, which I have here advanced as that of the Christian religion, all that has any effective value in human affections and motives will be found implicitly contained. Every actuating motive, and corrective virtue that can influence individuals or reform and exalt the social state, will be alone found in the Apostle's definition of charity: in the most literal sense, it "covereth a multitude of sins." Suppose it universal, and no moral evil could exist. But, in this wide sense, charity has little place in the heart of human life. It is a renewing grace to be supplied by Divine power, operative through faith, "faith that worketh by love." We have then, first to contemplate the nature and objects of faith; for no human affection can be supposed without recognised objects; to supply these is the office of faith, "the substance of things hoped for, the evidence of things not seen."

There is a very striking and profound fitness in this selection of faith as a fundamental element in a religion of which the main motives and chief objects lie so entirely beyond the scope of sense. That such a principle would be little likely to occur in any human philosophy or heathen creed, will be sufficiently manifest from a consideration of the very distinct manner in which the affections and change of heart are involved in the Christian scheme. No faith is essential for mere formal observance —for festive celebration—for mere conformity to acknowledged worldly interests, enforced by law, opinion, and education. There are natural inclinations for religious ritualism, so far as no change of heart is required. We cannot fail to recal the various influences which may similarly control the actions and character of men : how pride, and self-interest, and fear, commonly operate as the safe-guard of social life—what mean and low, and even wicked motives may tend to smooth its outer surface. There is, for earthly ends, a large provision of conservative restraints and motives; but the root and source, the radical corruption at the heart remains untouched : there may be much for Mammon, but little for God. It is when such changes as are expressed or implied in the evangelical precepts are to be effected on the moral nature, that this actuating element, by which alone effectual motives are to be supplied, becomes an essential requisite. Thus then may be understood the profound and prescient wisdom manifested in the adoption of this principle, while its necessity, still latent in all its ordinary operations, could not be distinctly recognised. "Believest thou I can do this ?"—"According to thy faith be it unto thee," was the seemingly needless formulary adopted by the Christ in all His acts of mercy. It was an inseparable part of the system, that all his acts were to be made available through this essential medium.

To see the full importance of this, we may take a brief

view of the principle itself; the more necessary, because the true intellectual operation of faith is liable to be confused with a lower modification of belief, which is the *bare assent* of the reason, and which does not necessarily convey *any* sense of reality to the mind, or any influence to the affections. Faith, which an eminent prelate* has defined as a confident trust, is the main operative principle of human motives. Without it the whole commerce of life would languish, and men would be as careless of their worldly concerns as most men are of their spiritual. From this it may, for a moment, seem that the selection of such an element should be rather obvious; but, on a close view, this will not be thought a just inference. Faith does not, like *mere assent*, come to the understanding as an inference *from consideration*, or *stated premises;* it has a settled hold as a conviction of experience; it is a fixed *habit* of belief—a latent element of thought and feeling, influential according to the nature of the object. And when this special operation is justly apprehended, it must appear that faith thus described has been happily selected for an end not otherwise to be effected. To illustrate this distinction:—A man has faith in results which have the sanction of universal experience, which he relies upon with a confidence wholly independent of any mode of rational proof. He may hold opinions contracted from education, with a degree of belief which, in proportion to his habits of conformity, may amount to the actuating principle of faith. But there may be an *assent* given to the main statements of the Gospel nar-

---

* Rt. Rev. Dr. O'Brien, on Justification.

rative, on grounds of proof similar to that which a student in geometry gives to some difficult theories, or in a rudimental acquaintance with some astronomical fact, without any moral result or realised conception. In this low assent, there may be many cases of a simple acknowledgment of a creed, without any resulting affection; the habitual operation is wanting still—there is no governing motive. There will be a deference so far as the world defers; a concession to opinion so far as opinion goes; forms are observed; decorum respected; compromises adopted; such is the religion of the world; the easy, but illusory "*safe side.*" But in all this belief does not amount to the dullest convictions which excite the industry spent on a farm, or which prompt the investments of trade, and must be wholly inadequate for the faith that is to influence in opposition to such things. How strongly is this illustrated in its requirements as stated by St. Paul—"For as you have yielded yourselves servants to uncleanness and to iniquity, unto iniquity; *even so*, now yield your members servants to righteousness, unto holiness." With the same earnestness with which you have given your heart to the sin and vanity of a godless life, now give yourself to the concerns of your salvation. Here, then, is the statement of a test involving the principle of true faith; earnest sincerity, and wholeness of heart. You must be a follower of Christ in the same wholeness of will that you are a trader, or a soldier, or a landlord, or anything else you are. And this is a true indication of the operative principle of that realizing and influencing belief called, in the Christian system, faith.

From this exposition it may, so far, appear with what profound propriety this main principle of action has been incorporated in the moral part of the Christian scheme. But it must be considered not by itself, but in its combinations, its objects, and designed operation. Separately taken, there is no reason why this or any moral element may not be included in any theory, moral or religious; we must bear in mind that it is the exclusive selection and place in a system we have to consider. It is the faith that communicates the *hope* in Christ—the faith " that worketh by love." There may be a faith that worships at a tomb, and a faith that lights the martyr's pile, and calls down fire from heaven. This is not the faith that fulfils the test of Christian discipleship, or recognises the sinner's hope. Faith is not to be considered apart from its proper object, and the combination in which the Gospel presents it. It is the instrument of the Spirit that works in man to will and do; to unite him with God in Christ, and to alter his moral nature by the hope and the charity that are, with it, abiding elements. It is to act not simply by inferences, but as a great alterative— not as an occasional motive, but as a habit and a change of nature. A man may sign a confession of faith and think no more of it, or be zealous to slaying, for a dogma or a form, without faith, or charity, or hope. He may, like the Pharisee, pray three times a day; or, like the same self-approving formalist, give half his goods to feed the poor. This is well, but not necessarily the fruit of faith. Pride and ostentation will do these things; men's failings may often lean to virtue's side. Faith has its own single object, and from this alone its proper motives flow. And this leads to a very striking result, relative to the mode in which its operation on human character, must become effectual, as evidence of " things unseen."

When we take into our account the invisible character of the actual objects of the Christian's faith, and the manner in which alone (humanly speaking), such objects can be reduced into actual conceptions, and qualified with influential power—it not only offers an added reason for the antecedent necessity of spiritual aid already inferred from experience, but also illustrates the effective fitness of the principle of faith as a moral alterative. For faith, in its truer sense, must be promoted and maintained by the continual employment or working of the means of grace; it is thus necessitated to become a *habit* of mind. And this is among its most rationally intelligible conditions: you can be nothing truly that you are not *habitually*. Hence might have been inferred, antecedently, that which is so strongly enforced in the gospel sentence, " Watch and pray,"—" Pray without ceasing"—a continual communion of the heart with the unseen—a constant recollection of an invisible presence.

But from this same consideration we are led to another most interesting fact. An antecedent requirement of another kind opens before us, and we find a still more surpassing indication of the all-provident wisdom that has done all things so well for man.

The objects of faith are " the things unseen :" neither heaven nor hell, nor the Omnipotent Creator and Lord of all, are reducible into any of the forms of human thought. The indications of Divine power can be traced by science in the heavens and in the earth; but for the mass of mankind there is nothing for the affections to cling to in the abstract omnipotence, infinity, eternity, and omnipresence of that all-ruling Mind. The signs are everywhere to those who can read them truly; whether in creation, laws of nature, or Providence. But had no further provision been afforded for human weakness, the system, otherwise so perfect, must, after all, have wanted any distinct conception fitted for the faith and love of man.

God, "in sundry times and divers manners," is said to have given sensible intimations of himself to mankind. These are easily seen to have been accommodated to the successive stages of human progress. The latter and more perfect dispensation in which the moral and spiritual machinery of the system were to be completed into their (probably) ultimate form, was designed to be conducted by moral and spiritual processes, without the aid of interpositions which would not be altogether consistent with the general frame of the plan indicated in the constitution of the world, or with the manifest economy of a rule by law, or with the discipline of motives operating through the conscience.

Yet, upon any assumption, the heart claims *an object*, and the claim of the Creator, contained in the "first and great commandment," renders indispensable somewhat more than an abstract conception of God. It would have been a daring stretch of human reason to anticipate what it nevertheless would ask—some concrete and embodied conception. But such is precisely what God has provided, by a most wonderful appointment, most inscrutable in its nature, yet most simply intelligible as a fact ; *God, "manifested in the flesh"*—the main and central object of faith, of hope, and of love.

Such is the Divine expedient which was manifestly essential in this important (though still subordinate) sense, by which ; while the indispensable condition of Divine justice was satisfied on the cross ; in the life and teaching of Jesus, a provision hardly less indispensable was made for the affections and an example for the guidance of man.

It is in the latter of these aspects we are here to consider this arrangement. I have in this lecture, hitherto, dwelt upon the main elements of the moral law; we must now contemplate the actual object for love and veneration—and the model character for imitation. Such a character—beyond imagination, yet still quite intelligible, as made known in the person of the Saviour—could not have been invented: perfectly human in His virtues and affections, yet immeasurably above the standard of humanity—human in affections, and Divine in gifts, in all things like as we are, " only without sin." It seems needless to point out the expediency of some high standard model, to embody in a human form the perfect exemplar of the restoration of man to the original standard—the image of his Creator, having the divine affections which were originally implanted, purified from the contracted sin, and rectified from the misdirections in which they became vices. That some such model might be *antecedently* claimed may be a question, but there can be none as respects the principle of adaptation hitherto applied. The want in man's nature thus divinely supplied, is clearly proved by the universal tendency of human affections to that darkest and widest departure from the divine allegiance—image worship. To worship something conceivable, if possible something visible, is the deep-seated instinct shown in many ways in the mind; and when first the original ordinance had sunk into loose remembrance in a rebel world, generated a thousand idolatries. Man, created to adore, could not live without a religion, and found objects more absurd and gross as he was further gone from original knowledge of God. Looking on this prominent tendency, a true philosophy might see the antecedent probability of some such adaptation—an object of religious veneration, still idolatry, if not God; hence, too, an antecedent presumption of the Divinity of our blessed Lord. This instinctive tendency, probably implanted for this, and thus applied, merits for its importance a little further illustration: it may be worth while to recollect how names (called great) are worshipped by parties, and factions, and the devotion of followers—how profound is the zeal of a cause! The cause may be evil, or indeed fictitious; the hero may be a madman, or a mountebank, or an incendiary; and still the dupes may be animated by good affections designed for better ends. They follow the apostle of a bad cause; but his name is haloed round with visionary lights of virtue; his evil aims have lofty names; the demagogue's pocket is labelled with country's cause, and homes, and altars, and other things for which good men would fight. The deceiver, thus masked with the features of the patriot or philanthropist—thus, like Satan, robed in garments of light—has been and will be worshipped by the world; for such is the zeal of a cause, the veneration of a name. So strong, even in its degradation, is the normal element, by which example, and the sympathy with what is truly noble, may raise and purify the heart, and such is the example to which the Christian's faith can aspire. Among all the thousand histories ever written, the memoirs of heroes, saints, philosophers, statesmen,—the portraits from the hand of flattery, or even the idealisms of genius—no approach has ever been made to the artless and simple portraiture of the Gospel. Without method or skill of composition (unless we allow for the guiding Spirit), without apparent aim, the Child of Promise is drawn with a force, truth, and reality worthy of the prophetic promise of four thousand years, and of the purpose for which He came—to break the bonds of Satan and disarm death of its sting. There has often been remarked in portraiture a simple and natural truth of expression, which the reality of likeness alone can give; such is the figure that stands before us, on the mount, in the wilderness, in the garden, in the judgment hall, on the fatal hill. Perfect and unmatched in its moral and spiritual beauty, as a unique sculpture from some master of Grecian art; solitary in its combination of all that was ever conceived of severe loveliness. Were these simple and inartificial narratives offered as a specimen of classic literature—an effusion of philosophical romance—how far would the critic place it beyond the lofty dreams of a More, a Bacon, or a Plato. These are among the highest names of moral wisdom—how flat and narrow-sighted and inapplicable appear their loftiest inventions, compared with that simple truth which, while it is beyond the philosopher's grasp, can be understood by a child.

For this we might quote the infidel whose singular eloquence and refined critical discrimination were in no instance so successful as in his enthusiastic eulogium on Jesus.* The atheist's heart expanded with the inspiration of genius, as he contemplated that transcendent ideal of unfallen humanity. For once the spirit of hero worship had a true direction.

Such is the remarkable adaptation of which the expediency can be discerned in the very misdirection of human affections. The corrupting love given to earthly objects can find a purifying object in Christ. With his nature, purified humanity, enlightened by the Spirit, can feel the sympathy, the veneration, and the love. The devotion so often wasted on a leader—an Alexander or Napoleon, can on more true and more heartfelt grounds be raised to Him who is the Saviour—the Victor of Satan and death—the Resurrection and the Life; by that faith which lifts the heart to a sure apprehension of perfect security, in the price that has been paid for man's pardon—by the promise in which he rests in the truth and power of a Heavenly Father.

Beyond this, all is, as it should be, mystery. Any scheme of human invention would go on, and still labour to construct lofty schemes, according to the imaginations of man—some reflection of human passion or ambition, or, perhaps, of the still more insubstantial dreams of philosophy. But here the light of real revelation stops; another state, another world, in which things transitory are to cease, can have little in common with the character of this perishable being. The characteristic indication of truth is in nothing more observable than in this for-

* Rousseau.

bearance; that a religion having for its *express* end the resurrection to a future life, offers no circumstance, and tells no more than is absolutely essential to warrant this hope—that no fleshly desires that fill the breast of worldly life are bribed, but, on the other hand, checked and discouraged—" whether there be tongues, they shall cease; whether there be knowledge, it shall vanish away." No resting place for earth-born fancy is left— " Eye hath not seen, nor ear heard, nor hath it entered into the heart of man, the things that God hath prepared for them that love Him." How contrary is this to any system of delusion!

I am, for the present, concerned with the moral affections of our nature, which are (in my text) combined with faith, and its essential results; but I must observe in passing, that I do not consider such influences to be exclusively moral. I cannot doubt the effects of Christian discipline on the intellect as on the affections. It would be quite superfluous to prove the direct connection of those two components of the mind; to say how the understanding becomes the slave of feelings and desires, and is warped and clouded by prepossessions, and enchained to error by fallacies which they engender. Nor is the intellect without its interest when referred to our view of a future state. The intellect, as an inseparable element of mind, must survive and have many eternal uses, some of which are not indistinctly implied in the Christian scheme. It must indeed often suggest itself among the aspirations of the intellectual believer, that there are high and glorious regions inexhaustible of ever-new attainment, in the depths of infinity and of ever-working power; that there is not only love to be felt, but wonder-working wisdom, and justice, and goodness in all its boundless branches to be venerated; that creation, which pervades the infinite, is not to proclaim its Author's glory to this frail world alone.

But charity, the bond of eternal union, the root of all moral excellence here, and the ground of the brightest hope hereafter, is to be contemplated as the first result of faith—" faith that worketh by love." It possesses a twofold adaptation; first, as the main root of all earthly virtue deserving of the name, in this life; and next, as the source of happiness and bond of union in the life to come. That it holds the assigned place in the regenerative scheme by which alone, man can be restored to an approach to the original design, or his world to its normal state, is easy to be apprehended; for this it but requires to weigh the apostle's clear statement of its conditions and moral results, 1 Cor. xiii. 4, 5, 6, 7; in which every human virtue, and every condition required for social order in its fullest perfection, is contained. If any doubt should arise as to the strictness of the enumeration contained in the texts to which I refer, a moment's reflection would dispel it. The answer may be comprised in a few words from the same authority—" Love worketh no ill to his neighbour." Love is the direct dissolvent of strife, envy, emulation, selfishness; the direct incitement to benevolence; and, in its truer and better sense, social virtue, the love of all. Love, in its spiritual acceptation, regards the souls of men, compassionates the evil course, and rejoices in the good; and, as a true faith, frees the heart from the over-pressure of the care for temporal goods, so love softens down and dispels the fierce animosities with which they disturb and pervert the courses of life. All social virtues which are genuine, are thus comprised in a simple and compendious system, The schemes of ethic philosophy are mainly occupied in culling the branches, but here the roots are planted.

It is also not to be overlooked how closely these essential elements of Christian discipline are connected, and how they work together; how a thorough conviction of the truths revealed, as it carries the affections to "things above," must loosen the bonds of the world, and thus remove so many incentives to evil, and cleanse the heart for the entrance of charity; how, as it more fully discloses the prospects of life or death, it must awaken sympathy and compassion.

The same pure sympathy which is so prompt in every emergency of known danger—the fire, the wreck, the sudden calamity, to risk life and limb, would be not less ready could the far more terrible and disastrous depths of the sinner's future be really apprehended. Life will be risked to snatch a fellow mortal from the edge of a deadly fall;—the precipice under the sinner's way, could it be for a moment seen—who could look on his gay and heedless tread toward its fearful verge, but with earnest pity—without the warning call, and the hand to succour?

So far, then, we may discern with the clearest certainty, in these two main elements of the Christian scheme, the elements of social restoration to the full extent they are allowed, by the antagonism of sin, to work. This result is, however, not the main or final design, and has its essential limits and its compensations in another and final end. For the present, it is enough to say that there is *no other* way for its attainment, for such is the clear inference from our whole argument. The tendency of Christianity, as respects social reform, is plain enough in the progress of Christian nations, due to its influences alone. Of this I have said enough.

The operation of these spiritual affections, in their higher aim, is on the individual. However we may look on the Gospel for social restoration; every man is to look for his own individual destination; to be judged in his own single self. It is the joyful hopes, that are imparted by faith and love, that we are to regard as their last consummate adaptation in the work of grace. In hope, there is a divine expectation, that is the comfort and consolation of all real earthly trials, which cannot be attained otherwise than as a fruit of perfect faith and love. The union with Christ, the presence of God, are joyful prospects to the heart of faith. They are brought home by spiritual grace to the believer's mind—to the merely assenting Christian they can only be apprehended as dim abstractions. But I think it more suitable to the argument of these lectures to take lower, though still not low ground. Every heart of human mould can, in some degree, conceive the ties of social affection, and the pain which cannot fail to attend their severance, and the growing desolation of the latter years of life. Nor is there any compensation for this most sad of earthly sorrows, but in the hope which Christ has left in His resurrection, and which Christianity breathes over the grave—the promise of immortality, the hope of reunion. How precious is this hope. Is any portion of it vain? The Gospel does not, for very obvious reasons, dwell on the reunion of earthly ties of affection. But are they without foundation in hope?

The Christian believer cannot, in this world, safely allow any love to interpose between him and Christ, whom he does not see; but when the vision of his Lord and God is perfect, the greater love will hold its own place. But let us look to the facts as they appear to reason.

If we adopt, as a fundamental fact, the essential immortality of the soul, and the consequent maintenance, in any future state of existence, of the same elementary nature, it will seem to follow that all that truly constitutes its nature will remain indestructible. What these constituents may be, mere reason cannot say, although probability may be found to lean to the affirmation of the will, reason, and affections. This, however, is a needless question at present, as it is our object to consider how Christianity bears on the subject. Love, says the apostle, is to be cultivated as the greatest of all, for it "never faileth." And, as I have shewn from a higher authority, it was to be a sign of discipleship in Christ. Now, to quote no further, it is not only the injunction, but the discipline, spiritual end, and result of Christianity. To "love one another" is a prime consequence; and the assigned reason is, that this love is to remain, when all else in life shall have passed away.

Nothing can be more inconsistent with this great truth than to suppose any end to affections, which it is a main use of the present preparatory state to cultivate and purify, and a main commandment to practise; and which are the main adaptations in the discipline of every Bible dispensation*—the first and great commandment, on which "hang all the law and the prophets;" the working of faith; the test of discipleship; instilled, taught on earth, because they are to be known in heaven. Well might one ask, why brotherly or neighbourly love, or married, or any true love, is so often and so variously inculcated and enjoined? why called the "fulfilling of the law" if the bond so hallowed is to be dissolved by a release from sin and death?—if the soul's translation were to be a change of that conscious identity, in which all its happier and more endearing memories subsist, which alone give life its value, must be sunk in oblivion? Not such, manifestly, was the Apostle's belief, when he forbid his followers to sorrow for the departed as those who have no hope, and promises their return with Christ. Thess. iv. 13, 14. Charity, then, is to survive in all its fulness, when all that is transitory shall have passed away; when, "whether there be tongues, they shall cease; whether there be knowledge, it shall vanish away." But the everlasting bond of spirits can never fail.

Here, then, is not only a high source of Christian consolation for this world's heaviest afflictions, but a beautiful exaltation of the sentiment most entertained by the truest Christians. They, whose affections are purified by faith, and exalted by spiritual religion, are conscious of an eternal tie—they are to co-exist, where no earthly chance can divide them, and can look forward to walk together on a path of sunshine without end.

* Deut. vi. 5 : Matt. xxii. 37 : Mark, xii. 30.

Enthusiasts have often doubted on this point. They have insisted that the love of God must absorb all other love. God has declared no such tenet. It would rather follow, "The love of God heightens all other love." His main lesson is love to all men. If such a notion could have any just application, it should be during the temptations of this idol-seeking world, when God is ever least thought of. It is here, where it may err, it should be forbidden. God never willed that the love which he enjoined as the highest grace on earth, should be cramped or extinguished when that which is perfect is come. There is no such limit in Scripture, nor is there any precedent in experience, or in the moral analysis of life. When a mother has many children, will she love their father less? The free charity of the immortal soul, unmanacled from doubts, misunderstandings, and jealousies, and from the blindness, selfishness, and contracting cares of this narrowed state, shall expand to the measure of its glorious destination; and, so far from losing all its life, gain new force—all its feelings and affections shall glow brighter within the atmosphere of love that surrounds the Majesty of God—the Father of all, who has commanded that they who love him should love one another; and, while he has given faith and hope to guide us through our earthly pilgrimage, has made love, the bond of souls, the one surviving light.

So far may be enough to vindicate the close adaptation of the moral system of the Gospel to its declared ends—its primary adaptation to the eternal, with its full potential efficiency for the subsidiary temporal ends. It plainly bears all the character of Divine authority.

The results of human reason, in laws and morals, are too well known to admit of question on this point. The scheme of Christian ethics (fully developed by its Author), of which we have here discussed but the principles, was manifestly struck out by one Mind, without study or logical process of human reason. Having its basis in the past unknown, its end in the undiscovered future; yet so powerfully casting on the present the one only light adequate for its restoration. And finally, a just consideration of this ethical standard will also strongly illustrate the essential character of Christianity in its main design and operation as a method of justification. A clear view of the law must tend to shew the utter vanity of any hope to find refuge in its fulfilment; shewing thus the necessity of that atonement by which the sinner is saved by the simple condition of looking for grace in the sufficiency of Jesus only, and exposing the absurd notion that this great sacrifice for sin can be aided or rendered superfluous by any mortal merit; thus, " by the law is the knowledge of sin :" thus may be explained the apostle's exclamation, " O wretched man that I am, who shall deliver me from the body of this death," and thus finally, the full triumph of the answer, " I thank God, through Jesus Christ our Lord." I need not add, how clearly may thus be seen the entrance of the narrow way, so often missed: the straight approach to Him who has *already paid all* for them who come in trust—who have all to receive and nothing to give.

LECTURE VI.

GALAT. III. 21.

"Is the law, then, against the promise of God? God forbid! For if there had been a law given which could have given life, verily righteousness should have been by the law."

I have hitherto had to ask your attention to a system of combined and closely adapted arrangements, in which the constitution of this world, the state and nature of man, and the general scope, announcements, and character of the Christian religion are manifestly fitted together, so as to indicate that both belong to one primary system of design. This connexion is traceable step by step, and link by link, from the beginning and through the course of time—so far as, considering the nature of old traditions and history, can be required; fully sufficient to sustain our inferences.

I must now offer some comment respecting a class of objections, which, being in the nature of antecedent probability, fall within the scope of this argument. There could not, indeed, be a stronger antecedent presumption in favor of the Scriptures, than might be drawn from a full view of the scepticism of eighteen centuries, during which not one argument has been produced of the least validity, or without the interposition of some logical fallacy or unauthorized assumption. Many are the baseless subtleties and corruptions of the first principles of reason which have been invented for this end. But the limited purpose of these lectures renders it expedient that I should take a more narrowed range. There is a class of objections, which are derived from unwarranted assumption in matters beyond human comprehension, important, because, to those who reject the authority of Scripture, they have no direct answer.

Of such objections some have great popular weight, because they possess the surface speciousness attendant on either conventional fallacies, or truths misapplied. These, though within the reach of the most superficial acquirement and feeblest understanding, are unhappily, from their nature, impossible to meet on either common or popular ground. The unwarranted assumption in such cases can be but denied, and the question rests where it was. The caviller who speaks of Divine justice as he would not venture to talk of human laws—of the empire of being as if it were a village—and of God as if He were a country magistrate—can only be told that he knows not what he says—" Thou thoughtest wickedly that I am even such a one as thyself."

When scepticism or dogmatism has recourse to assumptions beyond the sphere of sense or experience, and travels for argument or objection into the transcendental void—into the infinite and eternal—the undeclared attributes of God, or the nature even of mind—in either case the rash adventurer may be more fairly than effectually met by a denial, which cannot remove in all cases the influence of a specious semblance of logical reasoning. But in the treatment of such fallacies there will often be found to occur, an embarrassment not easily evaded : too often the exposition of sacred truth has led to a rash and dangerous use of the same fatal inadvertence, and truth has been as much betrayed by the error or ambition of its advocate, as by the inveterate audacity of its enemy—

"Iliacos intra muros peccatur et extra."

It is thus, that when we are led to the necessity of combatting the scepticism which offers itself under the sanction of a theological theorist, it may so happen that the metaphysical Divine sits encamped in the rear. Unqualified assumptions respecting the nature, attributes, or plan of God, into which good and learned Divines, of over subtle temper, have been at times betrayed, are accepted as admissions, by the adversary, and very differently applied. Reasoning on attributes of which, in their higher sense as predicated of the Supreme Being, no just conception can be formed,—or any notion in what way they may be modified by a supreme law, by universal expediencies, by mutual limitations; the Deist adopts the narrow assumption of some undefined rule of justice, mercy, wisdom; unlimited, and yet inconsistently taken in its most circumscribed human modification,—and reasoning from the nature, obligations, and affections of humanity, objects to Christian doctrines as inconsistencies, cruelties, and injustices. The error lies in the utter inadequacy of all human notions beyond "what is written," and even, so far, when taken beyond the strict intent. And it is for this reason that no explicit circumstantial refutation is to be opposed to such assumptions. Any reply beyond the appeal to human ignorance is likely to incur the risk of like error. We cannot quote the supreme statute; or state the motive of the Divine Mind; or measure its attributes; or specify the actual expediency; or shew the origin, beyond some declaration which does not go back beyond a recorded fact. Human comprehension does not reach beyond the limit of our present state; infinitesmal, perhaps, compared with the empire of which it is a little portion.

The most formidable objections of the Deist are those which thus rest on this mysterious ground, untrodden by human sense, and unexplained by revelation. Ordinances which have their origin antecedent to man, and which may, or rather must, have an essential connection with numerous possibilities beyond conjecture, are presumptuously compared and measured by the confined experience of things known. We cannot, in the case thus described, without equal presumption, meet such objections by any pretence to affirm the precise exigencies, causes, or laws of action, from which the state of things, or its origin, has arisen. But in taking such questions on the ground of the present argument, objections of this class may be very fairly put to the test of antecedent probability: they are (as I shall presently explain) liable to be treated as problems which are manifestly indeterminate, and which therefore must, so far as human reason is to be applied, admit of many solutions. The antecedent objector is, therefore, satisfactorily met on his own ground, if a reasonable solution, unobjectionable on the same ground of analogy on which his objection rests, can be found. We cannot thus pretend to a *certain* conclusion, for there must exist within the scope of being unknown conditions beyond conception ; but still, according to the strictest rules of reason we are free to answer the objector on his own ground : a solution may be looked for, to which, on his own conditions, he cannot object. When this is done, though no *new truth* is gained, the objection falls to the ground. For it must be kept in view, that the supposed class of objections are not so much positive affirmations of fact, as implicit denials of the probability or possibility of solution. Any solution, fully consistent with analogy, is a full answer.

This *empirical* method, of which, for evident reasons, I have endeavoured to give the most guarded statement, will be found available for several applications which cannot be satisfactorily reached by any other method. I now propose to apply it to a case most to the purpose of these lectures, and which will, I trust, have some interest. The sceptic's most effective and most popular objections apply to the whole of the doctrine and alleged facts immediately comprised in the history of sin and the scheme of redemption. His objections both impeach the justice, and question the power of God. I have to shew a (possible) explanation *entirely consistent with all known* facts, and *the entire analogy of experience;* so as to leave the *known* attributes of God untouched, and shew the probable existence of a broad and infinite scheme, consistent with all we certainly know, and not inconsistent with the majesty, and power, and wisdom of the Sovereign to whom all existence is subject.

In the first chapters of the earliest human history, we have an account of the temptation of our first parents by a Being, there figuratively described, but afterwards variously adverted to on the highest authority, and identified as a rebel spirit—the adversary of God, and the enemy of man. His purposes, also, and modes of pursuing them, are often circumstantially stated, so as, at least, to leave no doubt as to intent of the history, or of its several statements; while the antecedent circumstances and originating motives are left open to conjecture, and are placed beyond any certain conclusion. That there is an adverse Being of great though limited powers, that there are angels which kept not their first estate, is the record; but how the fall or how the enmity began is unknown. Nor is the special direction it is recorded to have taken, or even the immediate consequence, wholly within any full authentic explanation. On these consequences many sceptical objections and many philosophical speculations have been indulged. It may offer the broadest scope for our illustration.

The fearful Spirit to whom I have adverted is to a great degree ignored in our popular teaching. Partly, I suppose, from an apprehension left by the Manichean heresy; but still more by a mistaken sense of the strangely inapplicable associations of the ridiculous, with which profane humour has helped to disguise the Enemy of Man.

As I have said, the New Testament also warrants the belief that, with this formidable Being, there are others in league, and in a similar condition; thus (I would say) representing a considerable class of guilty and fallen creatures, in rebellion against their Creator, and under some law of condemnation, while otherwise morally free, in the same sense as this condition applies to man.

Further, we have the same authority for the existence of other classes of angelic or spiritual beings, living under the government of the Supreme Power, or Ruler of the universe. With these premises we may take all things of which we have sensible observation, as offering the observable, and, therefore, determining and characterizing portion of a universal system; and thus offering a rule of construction for the broad analogy in which the only rule of probable reason can be found.

In the account of the first temptation there will appear a very significant glimpse of some antecedent condition of things. Taking together all that in Scripture is made directly, and indirectly, to appear of the conduct and character of Satan, there seems to arise an obvious inference, that he must have been *cognizant of some strictly legal conditions, such as to give effect to the crime he was about to commit ;* and there must have been calculable consequences, not likely to be obviated by any immediate *arbitrary* interposition, or without setting aside some *fixed law*, or some breach of a universal established constitution. It is plain that if he had known nothing more than man assumes, he must have shrunk from a daring aggression, to our seeming so easily avenged and repaired: otherwise, nothing in the records of insanity can be supposed more purely chimerical than his conduct. We are thus led to a surmise (to be confirmed otherwise on scriptural grounds), of some supreme and over-ruling expediency, of some imperial law affecting the universal constitution of the world of living existence, of which this globe is a little province—a law maintained for the necessary subordination of all spiritual being—for the protection of a *preordained* plan ; a law, in virtue of which no evil can be repaired but by means in some way conformable to that preordained, perfect, and all preserving constitution, which is the immutable law of Divine jurisprudence. This is not improbable as an inference, on any scriptural grounds.

But the existence of some such system, is the independent presumption of reason grounded on experience. Whether on scriptural or general ground, we are warranted in the assumption of a wide compass of spiritual being; variously intimated in Scripture : it is in the highest degree the result of analogical inference. On this I must say a few words. No reflecting observer will reject the probable conjecture, that the boundless expanse of the material universe, which God has filled with light and order and unity of plan ; offering, so far as science can explain, most of the well-known arrangements of God for the accommodation of life,—traversed through all its depths by light, the singular adaptation of Him who framed the eye for its use ; that, I say, this vast immeasurable expanse, through which the wave of light may have been reaching our little orb for thousands of years, must be presumed to be the area of a living universe—the imperial domain of which this earth is a provincial district, and on no known or probable ground to be excluded from the universal jurisdiction.

Considering, then, the breadth and uniformity discernible in all things, it seems highly probable that all is governed as *one universal dominion*, according with a universal scheme of moral order, which (however modified for partial application) is formed on the most perfect and strictest common principles, such as must be necessary for the maintenance of the whole living system, and the steady rule of free intelligences having varied motions of conduct, and, therefore (in possibility), accessible to temptation. All this, though unknown, may not less be maintained as probable. It is but an *extension of known fact* and *principle*—the continuation of a series, of which the first terms are known. It may be rejected as beyond our scope of vision, but with this rejection the objections also fall to the ground.

These observations lead naturally to the application I propose to offer. The account of the fall of man, as also the expedient for his redemption, are impugned by the sceptic, as inconsistent with his notions of certain attributes justly ascribed to God, but imperfectly understood by man. A rational sceptic may feel himself silenced by Bishop Butler's argument, of which my opening general statement is little more than an expansion. But analogy may be shown to lead further to the presumptive possibility which is to be found in a consistent solution.

In the application of the principles of justice, there is, of necessity, an expansion according with the constitution of things and the essential principle of order. In proportion as the field of polity enlarges, as the interests become varied, as the powers to be controlled and the obligations to be enforced have a higher force and wider scope, the strictness and the securities must increase in force and inviolability. A family may be ruled by prudent discretion and gentle influence. A district containing conflicting tempers and interests, and offering numerous contingencies, will require more precise rules, more precisely announced and more strictly administered. Justice is the right application of these rules. If we suppose a large dominion, the moral forces thus supposed grow numerous and strong in proportion. Now it is obvious to the apprehension how, in the same spiritual universe out of which the conduct and motives of Satan and his legions may be probable consequents, the expediencies I have indicated so far may grow to a law of infinite necessity. For while we have no conceivable limit to possible causes and varieties of outbreak, there must, nevertheless, be an equivalent maintenance of order. Only suppose spiritual freedom, adverse motives, possible error, all tending to disorder, and thus implying the necessity of some unbending model, some strict scheme of criminal jurisdiction becomes a plain result. You may suppose a ruling polity containing a wide range of provisions for Divine beneficence; but among them you must not assume an unregulated and *arbitrary dispensing rule* which would operate as a law of universal relaxation: for such there exists no known precedent, either in the affirmations of Scripture or of worldly maxims. The notion is wholly unwarranted.

The sceptic is often heard to affirm that there is somewhat incredible in the sacrifice of a Divine Being to repair the consequences of a crime so slight—so easy to prevent, or to forgive, or to stay all consequences. It is hardly necessary to affirm, that on the foregoing principles of reason he is answered. They indicate a solution on a highly probable ground; but in the special case this may be pushed far closer.

I will not lengthen this disquisition by any special

comment on Adam's particular transgression.* It was *disobedience*. It was a violation of a Sovereign command, at the prompting of one who plainly could not have intended a light or ineffective breach of the Divine law. Now let us consider what was to be remedied by the Sovereign authority. I will admit that, so far as human reason can go, if it were to be assumed that there existed no purpose beyond setting right Adam's transgression, its antecedents and consequences were wholly included in the act as stated in Genesis, and that Divine wisdom could have had nothing more to contemplate in its policy than an act of disobedience; I might, on this assumption, grant that it would not be absurd to presume, according to the rules of human justice, that God might inflict some lesser penalty, and institute some scheme of discipline and spiritual aid, such as, in fact, the Christian scheme includes. But how little of the probable—not to speak of the possible—extent of the exigency is thus assumed. The sin was not, as the questioner assumes, the inadvertent error or the feeble lapse of a mortal man: it was the frustration of a newly instituted plan, in its very beginning, by a high Spiritual Power—it was a defiance and rebellion against the Supreme Power, it was a formidable *example*, in the face of all being, of the breach of express law. It incurred the penal, and, most probably, declared operation of that immutable justice on which the moral and spiritual order of the universe may depend. It was to be judged, to be counteracted, and

* Note E.

repaired in accordance with the essential strictness of that eternal, immutable, and infinitely comprehensive law. In a word, the constitution of being was to be vindicated. The idea of an immutable, *because perfect*, law leaves no choice of methods. So far, it is simply the extension of the analogy of human experience to the existence of a broader and more perfect state; it may be wholly wide of truth, but it offers the only admissible ground of reason. If the sceptic will reason on probability, he has no other ground.

We are, therefore, *in reason*, free to assume that no summary or irrespective regard to the mere circumstances, as within human comprehension, could be adequate to the whole probable exigencies of the case: but, when we allow for the prescient wisdom to which the origin of the universal constitution must be referred, there must be supposed, in that original constitution, some statutory provision for disorders of which the future probability was demonstrably certain. Some remedy of adequate magnitude, though wholly beyond mortal apprehension, must have stood from the first in the eternal canon. Such a provision should be one of strict necessity, and of proportional adaptation. So far, though it may baffle mortal apprehension, is still agreeable to reason.

From these premises a clear solution of the sceptic's problem can be derived. The law was vindicated by an expedient act of the immutable justice, of the universal and supreme polity of God. Angels and archangels, and all the tribes of Heaven, trembled at a sentence of which mortal law has no adequate conception. While with this, a manifestation of love and mercy, proportioned to the goodness and greatness of its author, struck wonder and veneration through all the realms of being; the mercy of God, whose love is over all His works, was equally provided for in the polity of Heaven. Millions of his own helpless creatures, whom, we are told, He " is willing to save," were to be rescued, so far as the Divine law could be applied. Peace and righteousness were to be reconciled: truth and mercy to meet together.

It will thus be observed that neither the sentence of the law, nor the redemption, is, in probability, to be measured by the immediate guilt or forfeiture of Adam; and that, whatever may be the reality, there is within the compass of analogy, and the known laws of reason, a probable system of inferences which will fully answer objections: for it must be observed that beyond this rule, there exists no ground for human reason; and that the analogy on which the sceptic pretends to object may be extended as far as the objection can be applied.

In criminal jurisprudence a law can be satisfied but in either of two known ways; penal compensation or personal expiation—in either case bearing some proportion to the offence or the amount of evil to be repaired, or the danger from impunity. Now in the case to be considered, the first is not within the criminal's power; the second does not reach the exigency, it is in no way remedial, it cannot repair the spiritual frustration. If I should seem to approach too nearly to the level of human justice, I must repeat that it is our only conceivable standard; as it also is that involved in the objection. All justice proceeds from a common source—and is here but applied to a province of the same universe; and as also it is essentially contained in the declared and promulgated ordinances of revealed religion, we are strictly warranted in this application. We are clearly within the limit of the universal analogy; and only carry back to the source of all law the uniform result of all experience. We reasonably assume a harmony of system, such as is to be discerned throughout the physical universe, to be similarly maintained in the elementary laws of the spiritual,—all proceeding from one source, and, in probability, having one purpose. There is, indeed, no antecedent reason why the elementary law of justice should not be *one* throughout every realm of being, though subject to those circumstantial differences which must be known through all. The magnitude of the interests—of the consequences—the power to be vindicated—that also to be subordinated—the temptations to wrong—may all, in their proportion, exact a more absolute and far-grasping law; and, in proportion to the risk, and the remedial possibility, prescribe some more exclusive condition of reparation. According to the hypothesis thus assumed, the blow aimed at Man, and intended against God, was, in the highest probability, directed against the moral stability of the universe.* It unquestionably brought forth a call on the love and mercy of God for His newly-created subject, and a strong necessity for the vindication of His own supremacy. A sentence was to be passed, according to law, on the adversary and on his guilty dupe. Of the first I need not speak. On the human transgressor the sentence of the law must have fallen. But that sentence contained *in itself* a triumph to the adversary; this was,

---

* Note F.

at whatever cost, to be met by some provision—some clause of counteraction against a manifest design for the frustration of a Divine plan, and would antecedently seem to require a combination of mercy with indispensable justice. Man's forfeit by the law was life; but his existence was included in God's plan: his destruction was the will of Satan, his preservation the will of his Creator. The immutable law was to be satisfied; justice claimed a ransom—man had nothing to pay: by the terms of strict justice it should be adequate and not a debt already due. A sinless man was to be found—a compensation rendered adequate by inherent claims on the treasury of grace, as well as by a voluntary instead of an enforced self-substitution. Such might be the law, such should be the requisition of Sovereign justice. God-like love interposed to meet the dread condition, and to redeem millions of immortal creatures, with a price required by law, and adequate to this glorious end. In this there can be found none of the cruelty alleged by the Deist; it was a sublime self-devotion far beyond mortal comprehension, beyond the measure of any standard but the love and pity of the Divine Sufferer. Let human reason turn itself in every way to find some less objectionable reparation, such as might meet the previous conditions of the case. An unconditional pardon would be a vicious example and abandonment of justice. From mortal condemned to all that mortal could undergo there was no room for more, there was no lower abyss to sink to; good deeds were but the common debt of all men; contrition and sorrow repair nothing, and satisfy no law, Divine or human, and, duly considered, could have no effectual existence in the present state of man. Some great expiation, some ransom of the most comprehensive application and magnitude, must, on any probable assumption, have been essential to repair an evil having its source in the depths of spiritual Being, its possibility in the necessary constitution of things, and its recognition in the primal polity of the universe; and, as it is easy further to discern, having a potential principle of expansion and accumulation through all ages and all worlds. A Divine expedient which, by the principles of eternal justice, could be accepted both as expiation and as inaugurating a new Divine jurisdiction would be a reasonable presumption; and though somewhat more than may be antecedently devised in its wholeness by human reason, is yet fully within the limit of probability. We cannot ascend so far into the heights of Divine policy as to conjecture upon special expedients; but, taking that which the record supplies, we can answer many specious objections. We are not permitted to assume positively many things which yet may be; but we cannot leave the sceptic to argue on the assumption of an *arbitrary and irrespective* will, involving no absolute conditions of reason, justice, or expediency. This would imply the needlessness of any atonement, on one supposition; on the other, it would imply an opposition between the first and second Persons of the Godhead. Were we, instead of law, to assume a wrath so extreme as *irrespectively* to award the eternal doom of man, it would plainly contradict our knowledge of the Christ, who claims unity with the Father, by ascribing to Him an *opposite will*. Nor can we assume the *mere* principle of intercession, for a similar reason; nor a Divine wrath appeased by sacrifice, which would, if literally understood, imply not only wrath against man, but some feeling to be gratified by the humiliation and suffering of the Son. These *are the chief taunts of Deism!* They are answered by the probable assumption of a prime original institution of conservative law which extends to all worlds; to be maintained only by expedients within its own comprehension, and to be applied seasonably by the wisdom and goodness that ordained the universe and its laws, and will not change, because all change would be imperfection.

Such are the antecedent presumptions. The statements of the record are not very different. There was a penalty to be paid by man; it was necessary to find a victim free from the yoke of an *existing* condemnation. But how was such a victim to be found? What son of Adam was unbranded with the signet of Satan, and undefiled by the contracted pollution of his kind? Would an angel be qualified to take this awful place? Could angel courage meet the fearful doom? It would be vain, it would not be for an inferior being to efface Satan's vaunted triumph over Omnipotence. Can reason cut this knot among the mysteries of the Creator? No; but guided by analogy, it can still descry the sublime truth and consistency of what is written. It informs the Christian believer that man, through the instrumentality of a being hostile to God, and in holy writ termed the Adversary, incurred a fearful sentence, and became degenerated into a state in which he does not exist according to the will of God; that he is, in certain respects, under the power of the evil being who has obtained this fearful advantage. We learn that God is willing that man should be saved, and that his love and wisdom has struck out the " one way," a way conformable with his eternal and immutable law. By this one way it will be easily apprehended how the requisite conditions are satisfied, how the love and mercy of God are reconciled with justice, the order of the spiritual universe preserved and maintained, the adversary defeated, and the irretrievable doom, which fell as a blight over a great province of God's dominion, neutralized by a terrible but glorious equivalent, the self-devotion of a Divine Being " equal with God as touching His Godhead," but in the nature and person of man, " only without sin."

By this Divine Person was the penalty paid, " He was bruised for our iniquities ; by His stripes we are healed." On Him was "laid the iniquity of us all." Such are the *data* of the record, fully accordant with our theoretic conditions ; and though, in this specific form, beyond the grasp of human reason, still perfectly satisfying its conditions.

Let us now pursue these doctrinal statements in their further relations with our analogical theory.

To make the satisfaction thus provided available, the Divine Redeemer took upon Him the nature and brotherhood of man. As man, He was tempted and tried, and being Himself free from the penal obligation of the law, had laid upon Him the debt of Adam's race. As man, He "fulfilled all righteousness"—the sum of mortal obligations. In man's character, He satisfied the law. As man,

He bowed before the throne of justice and power and eternal glory. As man, He suffered a vast and mysterious amount of agonies and sorrows—multiplied perhaps in proportion to the magnitude of His indwelling nature. As man, He entered the realms of death. As man, He rose to claim as well as to foreshow the resurrection of man. As man, He ascended to take possession in heaven for man. Reason cannot follow into that glorious inheritance so secured. But we can, without difficulty, apprehend the rational consequence. Man, evidently, thus obtains a *clear new title*, through the Divine mediation thus described—a claim of *Divine affinity*—a brotherhood on the throne of mercy and grace. He is removed out of the scope of the law into the limitary precinct where the law cannot enter. Here we fall back on our theoretic inference—is it presumptuous ?

Clearly as it accords with our theory, and agrees with our facts of record, yet had we no more than *inference* from either, we should not dare to say such things. But we have only anticipated the strong statement of the Redeemer's own lips. Let me recal these affecting expressions of Divine love.

Every one now present must, doubtless, recollect the affecting address of the Saviour on a memorable occasion. I quote its conclusion—" As Thou hast sent Me into the world, so also have I sent them into the world ; and for their sakes I sanctify Myself, that they also might be sanctified through the truth. Neither pray I for those alone, but for all who shall believe on Me through their word, that they all may *be one*, as Thou Father art in Me, and I in Thee, that they also may *be one in Us.*"

This language is very variously used by the same Divine Speaker, in such a manner as to imply some *unity* of no secondary import in relation to His connection with man as Redeemer. And mysterious as such a unity must be, it is manifestly agreeable to the previous assumption, to the recorded facts, and seems to convey the operation of a principle not unlike that already suggested by those facts. As the principle is not without importance, I may add one more instance in which the same idea is strongly conveyed by a figure of the vine and its branches, expressive of some similar meaning. There is, it is true, an inferior sense in which this passage, John, xv. 6, is understood. But, taking both passages together, they seem to convey something more strong than a mere corporate connection, and may, I think, be taken to convey that affinity which seems established by the mere fact of the Christ's humanity. We have some tendency, from habit and the declamatory taint of modern language, to be little impressed by figures of speech ; but (not to lay any stress on the dignity of the speaker) it is easy to see that, in the style of Jesus, they not only more clearly illustrate a moral or doctrinal truth otherwise requiring more length of exposition ; or, by comparison, convey an inference ; but are sometimes used to carry senses intended to be darkly conveyed—some portion of a mysterious truth. Observe the curious exactness of this figure of the vine ; the unity, diversity, and due subordination ; the root, stem, branches, leaf, flower, fruit, from the common stem, and transfused principle of life. How lively is the illustration of the spiritual system of being, beginning at the source of life and branching into the innumerable company of the ransomed of all ages. The fellowship,—with and through One,—of apostles, and saints, and martyrs, and those millions from many realms of God who are to stand at the last day on the right hand of the throne.

Nor will it be foreign from the purpose of this argument, to see the personal application of this glimpse of a Divine mystery thus not dimly offered. Are you truly in fellowship with Christ? You have obtained a new claim on a new covenant. The Gospel is not only a revelation and a law, but a charter of incorporation, your credential in the Day of Judgment. You have put off the "old man" in Adam and have put on the "new man" in Christ. Your death by the law is cancelled by your change of state in the Divine Unity. Thus the plain evidence, the sensible facts, the intelligible probabilities, the authenticated records, form the broad basis of the lofty pyramid which rises gradually into the transcendental height of a mysterious truth which it supports —a mystery of God. You need not understand it; it is the assurance and the work of Him to whose power all is committed in heaven and earth.

A somewhat rash, but deeply interesting question, was once asked of Him who alone could have answered such a question—" Are there many that be saved ?" This question might well have been suggested by the same circumstances which may often suggest it still. I need not now cite the reply ; but the object of my argument imposes it on me to take some notice of an antecedent objection on this ground, which is known to be much resorted to in popular scepticism, by the common class of disbelievers and doubters, whose objections do most mischief, because they lie on the surface and are accompanied by no reflection, while at the same time they extend common conventions of human opinion and the morals of social life to considerations in which they have no application ; thus, indeed, it is that " fools rush in where angels fear to tread."

From what I have now said, it will be perceived that I do not pretend to give much satisfaction to those who ask this question in our times. It is grounded on a fallacy common to the sceptic and a growing sect of Christian dogmatists, who derive their different conclusions from a common error. It is an error which ignores the greatness of the Supreme Being, and comparative inferiority of man ; the consideration of justice ; the worthlessness to God of any creature, whatever may be his assigned place in the scale of being, who revolts from that place, abjures its obligations, and refuses to be in accordance with the plan of his Creator. The error arises from the magnitude of the divergence ; the servant forgets he has a master, and thinks it unfair to condemn his neglect of service. One moment's rational attention turns these objections and rationalizing dogmas into absurdity. What, in Divine estimation, can be the difference of value between the human rebel and the meanest insect that crawls under a microscope. The unbeliever, who defies and has repudiated the only means in existence of direct knowledge of his Maker, looks round upon a narrow scope of a narrow sphere of being, invents an imaginary God, whom he only allows for the purpose of a sophism ; assumes rules of action unsanctioned even among men, and in his narrow circle of intercourse overrates himself. He has no conception of the Ruler of a million worlds, of powers and principalities, of creatures whom he would fall down and worship but that he does not see them. He has not computed what an atom he is in the infinite of being—what a grain of dust is the speck which he inhabits; it does not cross his brain that there may be a supreme purpose in the operation, machinery, and progress of which his being is involved—that his destruction may be no more than a *consequence* of his folly and guilt, the iron wheel of supreme law under which he has thrown himself in defiance. We cannot span the awful gulf between the present and the remote of being, from which just thought, humble in proportion to the grasp of its conception, shrinks back with reverent awe. The giant intellect of Newton only ventured to bow at a name so full of dreadly vast suggestion, and, with an affecting union of simplicity and sublimity, compared himself to a child gathering shells on the shore of the eternal deep.

It is to such vain reasonings that the profound observation of Bishop Butler so well applies. Christianity, as every system from the same Author, is a "scheme imperfectly comprehended;" and this our imperfect insight becomes in the nature of proof. A system in all its parts thoroughly explicable on grounds of human experience cannot have relation to a scheme of things beyond that experience.

I shall conclude by reverting to a fundamental consideration which I could not have conveniently followed out in the beginning. The sceptic has asked why moral evil can have been allowed by Omnipotent wisdom and goodness. This question, irreverent to ask, and almost as much so to answer, includes a compendium of false assumptions. I cannot here take space sufficient for its full discussion; but I introduce it to offer a suggestion which appears to me to have some value as respects the principle of the error. It will deserve a brief statement, for which I must ask your indulgence.

It might appear too curt and suggestive of error to say that the highest possible perfection may be, so far as reason can prove, necessarily connected with some possibility of evil. But let us look into the question. All sensible experience shews that God works from means to ends, and that his moral plan is a development of the more perfect from the less. Among these means the most unequivocally apparent are motives. All conceivable sources of conduct spring from voluntary motives, and imply a free choice to go right or not; virtue obeys in opposition to contrary motives, to which vice yields. Thus will be seen inevitably to arise the presumptive inference of imperfection; the essential possibility and, therefore, probability of moral deviation. Remove these qualifying conditions, and you have (so far as reason goes) a still greater imperfection—an inferior system of being; mind without will, or will without freedom; no virtues or actuating affections; a living machinery working by a spring which cannot be called mind.

The prevalence of good affections, of clear intellects, and of motives to goodness will, with the overruling care of the universal Governor, on the whole secure a prevalence of good over evil. In the infinity of visible spheres, there may exist instances without number, save to the eye that numbers all, of the most exalted states of moral order, in which the high ends of the Creator are beautifully realized—perfect obedience, charity unchilled, unswerving faith, realms of holiness and love. But still, where freedom is, evil may enter; where it is not, goodness cannot come.

The sceptic's postulate is beyond possibility and known precedent. Progress is the beautiful and interesting characteristic of a moral plan; it is the *actual* law—the great analogy of the *known;* it seems to be the favourite rule of the Supreme Contriver, His eternal care. Within our narrow span of vision, we may trace this plan as the comet's path is traced from and to the infinite; the orbit is soon lost to sight, but its nature can be discerned by the comparison of points. We may thus look back over the records of time at each memorable era, even to the present, to descry the links of connection between the beginning and the end : the course of Providence grows upon the eye, bearing onward the destined progress of humanity. Throughout, when seen as a whole, one aim appears ; sometimes dimly, often lost to sight, but still returning with a broader and steadier light, while no other combining or connecting line appears. The first record is the beginning of the one plan which alone runs through all times ; which reaches us as the broad foundation of our social state when it is at the highest.

It may be a satisfaction to the natural misgivings of fallible and short-sighted reason, to learn that our creed is subject to no presumptive objection ; that its antecedent probability is little, if at all, inferior to direct proof. Still such arguments might be carried too far, if put forward as disclosing what God has not revealed. We know a few sufficient facts, without the help of presumptive science, or the babble of modern verbal theorizing, and firmly founded as reason itself.

These you know by your acquaintance with their sure record; and it is to be hoped and trusted that they have, with the Spirit's aid effectually given, carried to many hearts amongst you the still higher proofs of experience —the inward light they impart to those who follow Christ.

CONCLUSION.

An intelligent perusal of the foregoing discourses will, it is trusted, help to satisfy the unbeliever, who fears to accept that which he assumes to be doubtful or antecedently improbable, that he is under a dangerous delusion—that, independently of its unanswered and unanswerable proofs (many, and each sufficient in itself*), Christianity is in itself the highest existing probability, the only solution of the known sum of things. Its evidences are conclusive, so far as reason can go; but as the unbelief of most men is not derived from positive objections, let me remind the sceptic to examine in his own mind on what ground it is his apprehension of doubt exists. He will find it to be that, which of all errors he would most deny—a prejudice. His mind is wrapped in the dream of the present sensible existence, and he can conceive as true nothing beyond it: his very trust in the present is a superstition. If he is possessed of intellect and of time to dip into the writings and learn the speculations of the sceptic and the rationalist, he will become aware of conclusions which, (so far as they have any sense,) are a hundredfold harder to admit than the utmost of the miracles ascribed to Him from whom miracles should be antecedently looked for. Such, indeed, is a fact that has helped to convince many.

Let me now venture, without presumption, to say that the main steps of the preceding argument may be

* Note D.

safely subjected to the test of a severe scrutiny. They are throughout, in the nature of an appeal to facts, familiarly known to all commonly educated minds in the present day, and may be taken separately as popular admissions. I could have added much, had I not been governed throughout by a consideration of the time at my disposal. If the steps of the argument shall be admitted, the conclusion will not be questioned.

The world itself bears witness, through all its realms of existence, to its own origin from an All-comprehending Mind; while all its arrangements, so far as the argument requires, indicate a purpose; the numerous adaptations for life indicate its more especial completion in the human race,* which occupies the main place in the known creation; and, by a whole system of natural provisions, holds dominion over all things.† Human history bears witness to and asserts the position of man, while it equally shews his transitory, uncertain, and wholly abnormal condition; and indicates the want of every adaptation to any final completion worthy of the design and the arrangements in the past or present state of human life.‡

---

* This inference, which is one of the main first steps of the argument of these lectures, seems to have pressed strongly on Cicero. "His quærat quispiam, cujusnam causa tantarum rerum Molitio facta sit: arborumque et herbarum? quæ quanquam sine sensu sunt, tamen a natura sustinentur. At id quidem absurdum est. An bestiarum? Nihilo probabilius, Deos mutorum et nihil intelligentium causa, tantum laborasse. Quarum igitur causa quis dixerit effectum esse mundum? Eorum scilicet animantium quæ ratione utuntur."—*De Natura Deorum.*

† Lecture I.   ‡ Lecture II.

With the same clear authority, all that is known of man, and the entire records of the progress of nations, manifest both the fact and the necessity of an original communication of some kind with his Creator; the absence of the essential instincts of life and self-preservation must (as I have shewn) prove the necessity of Divine instruction. The very existence of heathen superstitions germinating from some primary source; the known progress of error; the unbroken transmission of one religious tradition, sufficient to account for all without any discernible breach of continuity, and this one a main instrument of human progress in its highest advances; all seem to lead to the presumption that in this central and continuous element of civilization, the secret of man's destiny should find its true solution.*

To answer the conditions thus ascertained, a further and more particular inquiry into the nature and actual state of man is followed out, to find what antecedently should be the main conditions of the religion thus affirmed. From this it appears that the present state of man is a state of manifest disorder, irreconcilable with any idea of original design; and that, therefore, any true religion must distinctly recognize, account for, and offer a remedial scheme. For this, the atonement, spiritual aid, and the moral system of the Gospel are shewn to satisfy the essential conditions.†

With the higher expiatory provision for the redemption of man, some instruction and discipline for the moral reformation of his affections perverted by the

---

* Lecture III.   † Lecture IV.

"god of this world" was essentially to be looked for. Next, then, we discover a moral scheme agreeable to the nature, yet above the invention of man.*

If the combination of realities, from which these conclusions follow with all the certainty of reason, were to be by any happy chance offered for the first time to any philosophic inquirer, ignorant (as commonly happens) of the Scripture and its doctrines and facts, he would be likely to present the world with the sublime discovery of some faint reflection of Christianity. Guesses of the kind have frequently been made on far less ground of reality. Plato saw the necessity and predicted the probability of some revelation. But a fact so plainly authenticated wants, for metaphysical minds, the charm of speculation—for *conjectural* science, the boast and ambition of discovery. There is indeed somewhat too often manifested in the writings of the learned theologian, a persuasion that truth must be explained and proved in some philosophical way: the deist seems to fancy that the most unsettled surmise of any physical theory is enough to outweigh all known probability. Many seem to take for granted, that after a certain lapse of time old truth can be no longer true. It is hard to admit that such abberrations can exist; yet they may be daily traced both in the writings and talk of our time.

There is a point of some importance to be impressed on the miscellaneous reader of the present day. The Christian religion is assailed by side-winds—propositions seemingly innocuous, and connected with it indirectly, are insidiously and speciously proposed, so as to sap

* Lecture V.

the principles of faith. Some common principle imperfectly understood beyond its vulgar use by the multitude, is distorted into a fallacy, to convey a specious doubt :—some scriptural statement is, as in the "Phases of Faith," so wholly insulated and separated from the whole scheme of sacred truth, and from every consideration by which it should be understood—as to be brought down to some partial and inapplicable standard.

Every sophism which can have effective influence on none but the feeblest intellect terminates in some inference confounding Divine with human nature—some wholly unwarranted idea of God. Now of God there is no existing source of knowledge but from nature and revelation. If we take the latter, we must *take the whole record*, with all its disclosures—they offer various and opposite-seeming attributes, all uniformly converging into one well marked purpose : and to this all must be referred as the sole index of construction. God is the sovereign of a revolted world ; to condemn according to his justice, to recal, and renew, by counsel, command, instruction, and invitation ; and to pardon by mercy ; but mainly to restore the rebel race to his own dominion. In this everything will be found plain. Nor are we, in this contemplation, to neglect the fact that there is an adversary—a great revolting spirit working with guilty man, against the supreme order.* (Lecture VI.)

* This awful fact, in itself in the highest degree probable, and recognized in every form in every part of the Scriptures, seems to be strangely ignored in popular credence. What precise place it should have in Christian teaching I am not here concerned to say ; but I do not think any system of speculative Theism can be just or probable without it. I here subjoin a few texts which appear sufficient

The sovereign policy of God, taken apart from this design (as in much it must be) cannot be remotely interpreted. If we specify man as a rebel, as a frustration, as not according with his Maker's purpose, as forfeit and adherent to a rebellious spiritual power, he can have no claims on his Maker; there can, in justice or in reason, be no ground of mercy. His very existence is a blot—an interruption of a universal order—of which the consequence and magnitude cannot be known. Again, the purpose of God, as declared, is to recal and regain revolted man. Here, then, is the appropriated use of mercy, and here it never fails. Half the error lies in man's exaggeration of his own importance, referred to absurdly false standards. Human justice and mercy reject every rule that man would impose on God.

When a wide system of facts can be ascertained to reach through the entire extent of human knowledge, the inevitable conclusion is that in its direct and plain construction, so far as this admits of no doubt, it must be received as true. If in the wide range thus to be contemplated, *any part* is dark or uncertainly recorded, it must in reason be assumed to be (in whatever way) conformable with the whole. Now by far the larger portions of the Old Testament are historic records of the

---

warrant for the present application. Gen. iii. the Temptation; 2 Cor. iv. 4, the God of this World; Matt. iv. 3--10, Christ tempted; John, xii. 31, Prince of this World; Rev. xx. 2, Old Serpent which is the Devil; Ephes. ii. 2, Prince of the Power of the Air, the Spirit that now worketh in the children of disobedience; 1 Peter, v. 8, the "Adversary;" Rev. xii. 10, an "Accuser," &c. In fine, his entire character and offices are to be collected on proofs as clear as most other doctrinal statements of theology.

most authoritative character. Except the New Testament, no records exist having the same certain evidence as to their origin or preservation. With this their statements rise consistently from the whole previous tradition of the human race; they bear no character of fiction, of symbolic or mythical composition; they indicate a precise system of policy, reaching through many thousand years from Abraham to Christ.

Finally, it may be worth a thought to those who are disposed to listen to such cavils, that the main truth of the Gospel is wholly independent of all other considerations. It stands upon its own authentic credentials.* The birth, life, miracles, precepts, death, and resurrection of Jesus admit of no question, and are not questioned. Mr. Hume would have disproved them, and only succeeded to make it plain that, for this purpose, it would be necessary to prove that nothing else could be true, and to sap all belief even in the existence of sensible things, thus only illustrating the certainty of one faith commensurate with all certainty in nature.

"——————— If this fail,
The pillared firmament is rottenness,
And earth's base built on stubble."

* Note D.

NOTES.

NOTES.

NOTE A.

LANGUAGE—LETTERS—CIVILIZATION.

The sceptical theorists, on the kindred questions of which the subjects are prefixed to this note, may not inaptly be compared to builders who should propose to commence their castles at the summit and work downward to the foundation. Something must be allowed for necessity in many processes of historical research; but there must be a limit at whatever point all authoritative record ceases and pure theory begins. The antiquarian theorist may be allowed to proceed from such limits, to investigate the transmission and transformations of arts, languages, laws, and of whatever goes to the frame of social institution; but in all such theories the grounds are too doubtful and unsettled to warrant their extension to original sources. One practical glance at the capacities of the human mind, and at the history of its known progress, will be enough to expose the error of any attempt to derive any one of these first elements from untaught human invention.

The prime element of social existence, and of the first processes of reason, is to be found in language; without this nothing can be fixed on the memory, or introduced by thought into the simplest combination; deprived of this instrument, and without the instincts of the brute creation, man's condition must have been reduced to the lowest scale of brute existence, and incapable of any advance unless by means not at present known to have any existence. The brute of field and forest is possessed of instinctive tendencies wholly inexplicable by human theory, which are born with its birth, and, as by an inspiration independent of any known process of reason, govern its motions, and are plainly the gifts of the same common Creator, who has, from the first, endowed all creatures for their several states. This is the universal principle to be discerned through all nature, and there can be no probable reason why man, more especially the care of God, should be the sole exception. I have already shewn, on sufficient ground of fact, that man must have originally had, under some form, received instruction from his Maker; this conclusion, fairly considered, should remove all *antecedent* objection. It must be admitted that the prime element of all communication is language. The one pre-eminent capacity of man is, and ever must have been, that of receiving instruction, of advancing, *ex præcognitis*, in a course which begins in terms, in the generalization of which his ideas first become subject to the processes of reason. *No other way is known;*—all instruction begins in words which long precede their use as the exclusive instruments of human reason.*

The gratuitous attempts to derive language from imaginary processes, by their very extravagance and puerility of assumption, may well stand as an exposure of all such chimerical speculations. The most specious of these has

---

* There is a use of sensible phenomena, as signs common to man and brute, but this has narrow limits, and is not in question here.

sent man to school to the brute of the field and the bird of the air for this first rudiment of education. It would be easy (but rather trifling with the subject) to shew that such a theory, so far as it can be at all supported, could offer no suitable adaptation to the first steps of human advance. The bird and the beast may have been allowed to express by sound their own names; but language would still want significance for that lowest stage of savage life from which no progressive advance can arise: many subsequent stages should be taken for granted, to convert this mocking-bird dialect into the lowest process of reason. And I must here observe that such assumptions form too much the method of this whole class of theories: the conditions belonging to advanced stages of civilization are assumed as initial causes, and treated as instinctive tendencies. I do not mean to deny that many such tendencies must arise as results of reason and necessity out of different stages of social progress; but the assumed stage must have first begun, it is the first step is wanting. Commerce and law, and that favoured popular myth the social contract, genuine or ideal, have all their origin in states for which speculative casuistry fails to account, and sets aside for a description the exclusive property of the poet.

> "Mutum et turpe pecus, glandem et cubilia propter,
> Unguibus et pugnis, dein fustibus atque ita porro
> Pugnabant armis, quæ post fabricaverat usus,
> Donec verba, quibus voces sensusque notarent,
> Nominaque invenere," &c.

I go so far back for an example, because I think we have in these lines of the ancient satyrist, and a few which immediately follow, the most honest and undisguised example of this ὑστερον-προτερον method.

So far as respects language, the preposterous theories thus applied are the more remarkable, as the earliest record known suggests the only obvious and accountable origin.

In Genesis ii. 19, 20, we find a distinct intimation, which clearly implies the previous occurrence, or probably the immediate communication of language; the former is rendered likely by the special command mentioned, v. 16, which must have required some form of speech. It is remarkable that the process described consists in the acquisition of names, the prime element of reason. Here at least Scripture is coincident with probability. It may be admitted that the record is in some measure obscure and short of the requisitions of a social theory: but, besides that such was not its purpose, the nature and style of that ancient history is to be recalled. Whether by prophetic symbol, or inspiration, or immemorial tradition, the events of ages antecedent to history, or any form of record now known, are summed in the two first chapters of Genesis. Transferred from whatever source into written language by Moses, after a lapse of ages; and this, most probably, with no purpose now considered proper to history as a branch of knowledge; but for the assertion of the very foundation of ancient religion, the claims of God as the Creator and Lord of the world. Farther was not wanting, and farther no record then existing could go, to any purpose. Hence essentials are preserved, while numerous circumstances which a true theory of man's beginnings might require are wanting.

They who admit the only authority extant, cannot be at a loss as to the means of Divine instruction—for this no difficult interpretation is required; the methods are many, and distinctly exemplified in the Scriptures; direct communication; inspiration; visions; messages, &c. &c. each according to the special exigency.

As to the amount of primitive civilization, the facts are little known, but the probabilities are, so far as can be required, not obscure. They may have been measured by some regard to the wants of that initial stage of humanity; such arts as the preservation and comfort of life in some rude pastoral state should make essentially requisite. Some simple forms of religious institution must also be supposed. Some such seem to be implied in the sacrifices of Cain and Abel, of which, it must be plain on deliberate consideration, the notion could not have been suggested without Divine instruction. And it must further appear that the typical application of this ordinance to a remote event, and to the whole after theory of Scripture history, is as full a confirmation as can be required in a record so curt. The very assumption which may fairly be taken as an inference from the preceding argument, that a progress of civilization was to some extent designed, makes it reasonable to infer that a foundation was laid in a certain amount of instruction in religion, morals, and the arts adequate for such an end. It is easy to apprehend that, while no step in advance from pure ignorance can be supposed, yet very different stages of civilization may severally be sufficient for different steps of invention. As immediate results of what must have first been necessarily communicated, numerous mechanical resources of the simpler kind must early have offered themselves, and in the usual way have led to further art. Once the first steps are gained, there seems no objection to the assumption of a considerable and even rapid progress; such is the course indicated by experience.

But to this rule of progress there are limits as authentic. The early steps of art are rude, the fruits of necessity, and such as to be consistent with the state of intellectual developement from which they must be supposed to come. We could not rationally (were it not otherwise traced to its author) ascribe McLaurin's or Taylor's theorem to the primitive stages of human progress. Still more refined and complex, while also unassisted by the resources of a subtle science and regulated process of reason, would be the invention of the pure alphabetic method of writing. The analytic difficulties of such an invention have been clearly and fully demonstrated in a work of great research and singular acuteness of argument.* It is plain that this invention cannot have been later than the time of the Mosaic history; it has been clearly proved that no other record in which it has been used goes nearly so far back. Its previous use is negatived by the very existence (at later times) of ideagraphic writing; it cannot be referred to those early periods when people were compelled to find spaces for their writing on mountain cliffs and cumbrous piles of structure, at vast cost and labour, without some extravagance of assumption.

The pure elements of vocalisation subsist in a latent

---

* "Orthography of the Hebrews," by the Rev. Dr. Wall.

form of combination, in the words of every known tongue ; they are, in their pure and simple sound, wholly different from the word they compose. A word of four letters is compounded of four words expressed in one simultaneous sound, which it would, without the help of previous acquirement, task the most cultivated genius for analysis to decompose. Nor is it likely that so very subtle a discovery would be left without its record. Let it be observed to what it amounts. It necessarily begins with the conception of this as a principle—that the articulations of the voice, which can enter into language, have a limit, and must be followed by the subtle and highly embarrassing process of separating those elements, so that they might be recomposed in all possible forms of combination. Such is the character of the Hebrew writing, the earliest known : but there is no trace of the powers requisite for such an invention in the history of that gross and sensual race. Going further back, the evidences on the other side are far too strong. The very fact of a more recent transition of Egyptian picture-writing into alphabetic writing, long after alphabets were known to their Grecian conquerors, helps to fix this inference.

From the early periods of human existence to the time of the Hebrew settlement, the state of civilization was manifestly low. And going a very little further back into traditionary periods, there might easily be collected probable reasons for the affirmation of a state of barbarism, not amounting to the entire degeneracy of the savage state, but such as to warrant the assumption of a low stage of prior civilization. Such an inference agrees well with the general impressions derivable from the statements of Genesis. If we look for any sign of what such pristine civilization might be, our indications must be found in the remains of ancient art. It is nearly self-evident that the institution of the first rudiments essential to a single step in advance must imply the use of certain mechanical contrivances, which, though very simple in their nature and use, are dependent for construction on very refined principles, not within the reach of savage man. I have already said enough to shew the necessity of instruction in man's first stage of existence, and if this be allowed, it needs no elaborate analysis of the first elements of the physical conveniences of life, to refer them to an origin in itself the most probable. We are freed from all perplexity, such as some have thought to be connected with those indications of an early unrecorded civilization: all seems to indicate civilization to have been the pristine state from which, from many assignable causes, a degeneracy, more or less rapid in its local results, early began to set in; in some places retaining the element of progress, in perverted forms, and subject to perverting conditions; in others falling below all possibility of advance. Such should be the theoretic view derivable from the *entire* combination of historic, traditional, and local facts.

The first inference from this whole view leads to the plain conclusion; the *origines morum et artium* of social theory are not consistent with any view of reality, and cannot be referred to the savage state assumed by such theorists. If the question offers any difficulty, it is not, certainly, in those remains of a pristine civilization, which we cannot consistently suppose man's Creator to have neglected, without which he should have been inferior to the beasts of the field. We cannot assume that God created savages. The reasonable assumption from all else in nature is, that the broad basis for the social structure was laid in the beginning, and its indispensable conditions fully provided.

From this the several true aspects of man's history, offered by all admissible records, seem naturally to arise. There should antecedently be looked for, states of high but perverted social advance, coincident with false religions, but still emerging out of immemorial recollections and a distorted tradition ; while others might be found preserving local remains of early civilization more nearly combined with the simple forms and faith of true religion: and lastly, states of barbarism and degradation, the result of the adventurous emigration of families, such as have always existed in every nation, poor, untaught, into wild and desolate lands, and falling into the wants and emergencies contingent on such a condition. But assume this last to have been the initial state, and no progress could ever of itself begin; the first step is wanting. The vain inferences drawn from the study of ancient authority or speculation on these points can properly have no place in this note. The reader may find in Stillingfleet's *Origines Sacræ*, book iii., collected to his hand, the substance of many ancient writers, and many speculations upon the probable steps of the transition we have here differently arrived at. The sceptic who erroneously sets reason above authority is invited to consider the foregoing arguments. One well reasoned statement in corroboration of these views shall conclude this note :—" When we dismiss for a moment all antecedent conjectures, and look around us for instances, we find, I think I may confidently affirm, no one recorded of a tribe of savages, properly so styled, rising into a civilized state without instruction and assistance from people already civilized."* The same eminent reasoner considers the " use of letters" to have been an indispensible pre-requisite for such an advance, for without this, he justly observes, there could have been " no accumulation of knowledge." In this, too, I partly concur. It is plain, from what I have already stated, that such a requisition could not have been supplied in any spontaneous advance from the savage state.

NOTE B.

THE JEWS.

I do not know if any writer has ever distinctly noticed the central place held by the Jewish nation in the history of mankind, filling the whole distinguishable field of view between the antediluvian and historic ages. They are the first people in the annals of the remotest tradition, in any substantive form. They are the first by ages that have a written history. In their written records humanity first emerges out of the haze and mist of vague and visionary fable. The records of distinct and guarded family descent, in a cultivated language, a well organized,

---

* Introductory Lectures on Political Economy, by the Archbishop of Dublin : Fellowes, 1832, c. 5.

political system, stamped with the plainest marks of the Divine origination, which the whole purport of those records claims, all contribute to ascertain the place they hold.

In tracing the continuity of the religion handed down from the beginning, through their records, the clearest testimony of its true character, in this respect, is to be most fully observed in the successive steps of the construction of their singular institutions. The subject should have occupied a main place in this argument, had I not been tempted to bring it forward in a separate form, in a discourse formerly delivered before the same audience. As the foregoing statements without it are, in some degree, defective, I shall offer a few further remarks here, with a summary repetition of the most decisive of those offered in the former discourse. In the continuous and closely connected line of Hebrew records there is not alone a regular progression of events, tending to a remote result, but there runs through the whole a clearly perceptible thread of intent—a manifest contemplation of remote ends in a distant future. With this, there is the indication, at every step, of a hand not human, a will guiding and controlling in direct opposition to the current of all human tendency—a solitary instance in the progress of events, of human priests and leaders, people and kings, all passively moved forward to an unconceived destination by an unseen hand. If we carefully scrutinize the history of the most organized systems of human polity, it becomes easily apparent that they have not, in any way, resulted from any settled plan of governing wisdom, but (so far as human counsel was engaged), have been results developed from the unforeseen and unintended turns of social combination and economical causes; of wars, of errors, of crimes, of anything but human design. And further, that they have ever followed those laws of progress or decline, conformably to certain natural laws of occurrence. The one exception to all this is the history of the Jewish polity, in the formation of which every distinct step is discernibly adapted towards a remote end, wholly beyond the apprehension of any human mind, during the course of 500 years, and when attained not even then understood. Each of these steps had in it somewhat so wholly uncomformable to any human purpose, that nothing but the subjection to some over-ruling power would have enforced it. The people discontented, ever striving, were awed by fearful judgments; the leaders subject to the sternest self-abnegation; the kings placed under still more strict control; all without any trace of any human tribunal or civil jurisdiction adequate to such ends. We know enough of tyrants, and legislatures, and courts of criminal jurisdiction, from the Inquisition to the Star Chamber; in all these cases there existed known means and instruments of coercion. Monarchies have been upheld by armies and revenue, sometimes by the ignorance and depression of the people, by intestinal divisions, and other social causes too long to enumerate. The Jews had no tyrants who were not themselves under a more vigilant supervision and control; they were under no laws which it was any ruler's private interest to enforce. Only think of one usual human motive which prompts ambitious policy, and you light on what was wholly absent; talk of any source of power, it was wanting. The very record so carefully written and preserved in the face of that proud people, would have been fiercely suppressed by any other nation. Ever striving and still subdued, their history is unaccountable till we contemplate the recorded means and the known intent.

First organized from a family to a great people, by a succession of steps wholly distinct from human counsel, through a period of 500 years, compelled to move and rest, to toil and suffer, by miraculous visitations, in such a manner that miracle alone could compel ; the nature of the controlling power is proved by the nature of the submission. They rebelled ; the plague was begun ; the earth opened. The leader fell into a seemingly slight inadvertence ; a painful sentence cancelled his dearest hopes. The king took upon him an unauthorized step ; he was sternly reproved ; he failed in carrying out a Divine command ; he was sentenced to the disinheritance of his line, not by popular will, or any human power, but by a judgment whispered to his private ear, and executed by the hand of Providence.

In the great empires of ancient and modern times we may trace the successive occurrences and casualties which have combined to work out the resulting polity. But in each of these steps there will be found no trace of intent ; no mark of art or skill ; no sign of the end in the means. On the contrary, in the erection of the Hebrew polity all is as the stones regularly carved and squared, the pillars, and arches, and aptly planned elevations for the edifice and its ends. The materials, too ponderous for human hands, are framed together by the only adequate power.

" Now the entire of this course, if attentively followed from the first call of Abraham to the hour when Moses looked from Pisgah on the land he might not enter, indicates in the plainest and most unquestionable form, on the testimony of most authentic records, all the essential characters of a well and precisely arranged plan, highly complete, wonderfully adapted and harmonized in its parts; while every part is still wholly distinct from any of the known normal methods of human contrivance or social change; and, also, so little perceptibly connected with the remoter results as to be wholly beyond the reach of any human policy. During that long chasm of ages in which all hope lay buried, no moral prescience could reach through its many singular and unparalleled vicissitudes, from the call of Abraham to the mighty race that at last, in the end of the predicted period, crossed the Jordan into the land promised to their ancestor. The intent is yet traceable throughout, nor (when the whole result has passed before our eyes) is there a single step of which the contrivance is not as intelligible as the most exactly traced succession of historic events or the best arranged civil ordinances. The command to Abraham—the sale of Joseph by his brethren—the years of famine and plenty—the consequent migration into Egypt—the slavery—the release without force of arms—the sudden, and humanly impossible, arrest and forced return of that wilful multitude from the very verge of the promised land—all, and this without any express consideration of the means, form the well harmonized train of steps to a definite end, not one of which (unless by inspiration) could be antecedently referred by mortal to its real intent, or true place in the plan. The whole is one great miracle in itself. A further glance indeed must serve to disclose the fact, that not one of those steps could by any possibility have been carried through, unless by those direct interpositions to which they are ascribed.

"It has been the dexterous artifice of the sceptical philosopher, to ascribe extraordinary sagacity to Moses. But it would be impossible, among the many heedless fallacies of human philosophy, to find an instance more glaring of the utter disregard not only of the actual facts, but also of every known principle of social movement or economy. The order and economy of the entire of this long succession of steps were not only beyond the intelligence of its adminstrative conductors, but, though wonderfully adapted to its final attempt, wholly contrary to every essential principle of administrative policy; nor could it by human means have for one year held together that ill-cemented mass of turbulent and self-willed democracy. It was as a thunder-cloud rushing against the wind—a signal course of operation against the laws of nature. There was not one of the normal forces of social change in ordinary action, no old popular superstition, no established civil force, no appeal to passion or public interest—all was the stern authority of a relentless will. Moses not only possessed no known instrument of power, but was plainly shut out from every usual object for which power is sought by man. He was the first victim of every popular freak, and nothing could be more helpless than his position on frequent occasions. He held no weapon of offence or defensive muniment—no friend or partizan—no army—no body-guards—no criminal jurisdiction, or power of life and death—or chain and dungeon. No earthly protection stood between him and that fierce race; yet even a slight murmur was not allowed to go unchecked, by no vague threat, but by an instant recourse to means which, if not genuine, could have no effect whatever. The punishment was such as to leave no doubt of the hand from which it came. Moses fulminated no vague anathema from the altar, to shake the heart of the ignorant and superstitious—he carried his complaint to the ear that "heareth in secret"—prayer was his weapon; we find no trace of the dungeon, the axe, or the cord; but the earth opened, and the plague was begun. The insidious eulogy is simply absurd—the policy ascribed to Moses required real and perpetual miracles. It was no policy of man—nor can any earthly policy be found in its aims or in its event. Human history offers no parallel. It is easy enough to find cases of ascendancy won by popular seduction. The ancient resources of the demagogue are too familiar to be mistaken—the Mosaic institutions very remarkably exclude them; they leaned as heavily on chiefs and leaders, on kings and judges, as on the people. They assigned no privilege such as pride or ambition invariably seek—they conferred no estate, and hardly personal protection, upon rulers; while, at the same time, so far as the main design was not risked or in question, they had all those mild and temperate qualities of mercy and equity, which without supernatural power would have been wholly impracticable under the circumstances. The whole code was such as no human power could have introduced or sustained. The kings rebelled, and the people rebelled, but in each case the punishment came direct and immediate from the same high hand. You may scrutinize the records of Leviticus and Deuteronomy, and follow the history of Kings from Saul to the Captivity, and find, if you can, a line to favour any human ambition, or any trace of kingcraft or priestcraft, oligarchy or democracy. Nor will you find even, what might consistently be looked for, any very clear indication of popular devotion to a high cause—there was not any sympathy or enthusiasm to explain the submissions and renunciations of that strange nation.* They lived for a purpose which they did not understand, and which cannot be explained out of human statecraft. A dim futurity hung over them, faintly illumined by the gleams of prophetic vision; but it is only when we can look back with the full intelligence of many fulfilments and of the whole mass of events, that all becomes plain; that the uniform track of the real intent becomes visible to human observation."—*Act Sermon.*

NOTE C.

THE SOUL.

If we apply the condition of adaptation, as heretofore in the foregoing argument, to the question of future existence, its antecedent probability will seem placed on very strong grounds. These are, indeed, so prominent,

---

* " Much of this may be understood by recollecting the entire absence of every form of self-government the control was so absolute as to leave no room for *will.* No political tendency was called into action."

as to have been observed by moralists and poets at all periods. If we look on the nature of man, with a view to discover some deep seated ineradicable instinct, the most universal affection that may bear the name would be the constant projection of the mind into some futurition. With the lower classes of animated being, we have apparent facts enough to shew that hope, if it may be so called, is terminated within the reach of physical perceptions, and grasps no further than its visible object. Man's mind is, in all its aims, bent on days, or months, or years to come, and when it rises into the working of its higher powers, shoots forth into periods far beyond its earthly future. One of the forms of this strong tendency will be enough for special notice—the desire for posthumous remembrance.

Of this strong bent of human feeling there are costly proofs left from all the ages of time—picture and "storied urn and animated bust," and splendid monumental ruin; frail memorials that soon forget their solemn trust. Hence the heroic aspiration—" Victory or Westminster Abbey." Hence the imaginary life of the tomb—the strong ineradicable sympathy, with which the soul follows its cast-off frame of the flesh into the earthly cell of death.

The impression of an obscure superstitious instinct respecting the spirit of the dead, seems to have prevailed at all times in every age and nation; unsupported by any authentic reality, repressed by education, resisted by common sense, it is childhood's first terror; and still, after the powerful exorcism of reason, continues to walk the night and haunt the quick imagination. It would be a vain attempt to exhaust the speculations and superstitions of antiquity, which indicate the existence of this natural superstition of the human heart. Somewhat may be ascribed to the vague recollections of a pristine faith, but this will but dimly explain the many deep seated indications of this tendency of soul—the universal quest for a home for the spirit released from its earthly mansion—Hades, the Elysian fields, the seat of departed heroes among the stars.* All superstitions not immediately traceable to perversions of creed are in some way connected with the sense of a world of the dead, and an existing state of departed spirits; all vague, morbid, unsatisfactory, tending to fear, and to no hope, till touched by the transforming ray of " the day star from on high."

Faint and dim as such indications are, they manifest in some degree the nature of a race of beings created not to die wholly. The spirit, ever striving forward into an unknown existence, though striving ever in vain until taught by a surer guide than reason, manifests a Divine adaptation, a native constitution for eternity.

But there are in man's nature more living signs. There cannot fail to be observed a principle of intellectual growth, to which, during life, there seems to be no term of completion. The soul sits unimpaired amid the body's decay, still retaining its collected stores of acquired wisdom, yet far short of its completion still. Of this some specious exceptions may be offered. They however have no real weight. The laws of being are complicated among themselves, and can only, in many cases, be dis-

* Somnium Scipionis.—*Cicero.*

criminated or separately measured by extreme results; the assumed exception only indicates the interference of other forces. An extreme case ascertains the law. In the present life, body is the instrument by which mind acts; it controls and is controlled. And thus, in the variety of disorders to which the flesh is subject, it may so act on the spirit, or so fail to obey, as to arrest or derange its functions. The spirit's independent being is proved by the aged wisdom, eloquence, and grave judicial wisdom not unfrequently shewn in the senate or the judicial bench; modern times are not wanting in cases to illustrate the story of the Pylian orator,

> Τοῦ καὶ ἀπὸ γλώσσης μέλιτος γλυκίων ῥέεν αὐδή·
> Τῷ δ' ἤδη δύο μὲν γενεαὶ μερόπων ἀνθρώπων,
> Ἐφθίαθ'——

The soul may be cramped or disordered by corporeal disease from countless causes, but a Lyndhurst or a Pennefather are but instances out of many to prove its independence of them all; that, however its being may be momentarily obscured by the casualties and complaints that "flesh is heir to," its essence is untouched by the decay of its corporeal dwelling. The body may pass through its stages of life, and follow the physical conditions of decay, and the mind, in even numerous instances, hold its state unaltered, if not improved in power, with a manifest capacity of indefinite progress,

> "'Till old experience doth attain
> To something of prophetic strain."

It is a generally admitted result of all moral precepts, and all philosophic theory that has been received by the world, or has any confirmation in experience, that in proportion as men grow wiser, better, and more approved as examples, they have ever shewn a less clinging regard for the pleasures of sense—the gratifications of pride, vanity, and acquisitiveness. That the bonds of the world have been ever known to have a looser hold, and that if justly seen, such examples appear as the progress of humanity towards some further and higher state. Wisdom and goodness thus appear in the extrication of the soul from those things which are the most attractive objects and main goods of this temporal state. With this may be taken into view the great pervading conditions of vanity, uncertainty, and disappointment in life and its concerns, so that the world offers nothing proportioned to the desires, capacities, or potential exaltation of the soul.

The ancient philosophers have used arguments, often repeated by their successors in later times, resting on speculation, concerning the nature of the soul, or what may be termed the psychological principle. I cannot (after much reflection) attach any value to such speculations. There is some seeming of important truth in the proposition held by Plato, Aristotle, and Socrates, that the only known originating principle of motion is mind; it seems to be confirmed by observation—and follows no less from the received doctrine respecting the Creation. It leads by direct inference to the independent and permanent existence of mind. I must, however, say that the assumptions of those who have attempted to argue from the material or immaterial constitution of the soul, will not bear examination: all such theories are groundless, and unwarranted, so far as *positive* inferences (as in the case of Brown) are attempted to be drawn. There exists not the slightest presumption as to what the soul is or is not, in its essence, further than this, that the attributes of mind cannot be discerned among the known properties of matter. No positive conclusion follows. Bishop Butler has stated the right conclusion, which is strictly negative—there seems no reason to infer that the decay and decomposition of the body proves the dissolution of the soul. The rest of the argument is of no value. It is dangerous to use arguments of which the worth is so questionable. A very eminent living writer has very strangely illustrated this. He writes in defence of the evidences, but endeavours to shew that they can have little value unless the immateriality of the soul is first proved. Of such reasoning I would say, " Defend me from my friends." I have no objection to admit the immaterial nature of the soul—I must deny the *proof*.

The final and conclusive proof of the soul's immortality is, that life and immortality are brought to light in the Gospel, and thus stand on proof that leaves no room for reasonable doubt. That this proof is corroborated by very plain moral indications, by peculiar adaptations, is satisfactory to all thoughtful and observant minds ; and it is not to be denied that such signs raise a strong antecedent presumption in favour of religion.

The soul is manifestly, as light is, a *singular existence*, a thing *sui generis*, of which there are indications throughout the visible creation. Order, arrangement, contrivance, motion, growth, all are its influences and operations. Unconfined in expansion, we need not assume it limited in operation, or in time. There is enough of probable proofs in all we see, that mind is the eldest of existing things, and therefore an uncompounded, original source, permanent in itself and in its nature. Nor are we without some very curious indications of a different kind, in some manifestations of disease affecting the mind. I refer to certain well-known manifestations which appear in cataleptic diseases, whether naturally or artificially induced. Of these, abundant information may be found in a volume of considerable research and authority,* and many curious and interesting facts have since been brought variously into public discussion. From the general style of this discussion, I should be reluctant to dwell more specially on this topic. Omitting, however, much of which I have personal knowledge, and taking simply what is admitted on uncontradicted medical testimony, I may observe that, among the phenomena of a too well-known disease, there are plain indications of mental developement, manifesting intellectual operations unknown in the healthy waking state; modes of perception not traceable to any bodily sense, nor to be accounted for in any way satisfactory to reason. I here make no allowance for philosophic explanations, which, if they do not deny facts which cannot be explained, proceed on the notion that some explanation must be found for all things. But there is an inference of much interest independent of all theories. There must be inherent in the structure of mind, some powers unconnected with its present state of bodily combination, not given for the uses

---

* Abercrombie on the Intellectual Powers.

of its present existence; and looking, as in reason we must, for some intent, we can only find this among the provisions for another future state, in which other faculties will be required for other modes of existence. Nor is it a light consideration that these cataleptic phenomena not only indicate perceptions specifically different, but vastly more extended. If the facts be allowed, the inference is inevitable; the soul has in itself provisional faculties, the embryo of a more enlarged being, shut up, like the chrysalis, in this imperfect transitionary frame, and to be expanded into a new frame of existence by its release.

Among the anxious doubts which sometimes fall heavily over the strife of unsettled faith, perhaps the most distressing is the vain and not very wise effort to conceive the duration of any portion of our being after death.* Mere reason may explore the senseless dust; it can reach no further; the secret is not to be found there. Happy it is that He who has constituted the soul to live beyond the grave, has given a full satisfactory assurance to all who seek it where it is to be found. The proof is in its nature the clearest that human reason can receive, and on the surest testimony. They who entertain no doubts on the general evidence of the Christian religion commit a grievous error, when they turn from the truth offered for their faith, to find a satisfaction not designed in its remoter and more mysterious consequences. To such an error many are betrayed by the natural fear of death.

---

* Nescio quomodo, dum lego assentivi; cum posui librum et mecum ipse de immortalitate animorum cæpi cogitare, assentio omnis illabitur.—*Cicero Tusc. Quæst.*

It is but too natural, when man looks forward towards the approaching point of time when he can see no indication of his future, but simply apprehends that he is to pass into the void of seeming nothingness, and vainly strives with the dark doubt. In this 'tis wise to recollect that reason can give no light; that *it* is not the light given. How much better and more satisfactory is the assurance that is given from Him who made the soul, who must know His own work, and His own design, and the meaning of His own promises, and His own power to perform them.

These doubts were long ago foreseen and guarded against by Paul the Apostle. " Now if Christ be preached that He is risen from the dead, how say some among you that there is no resurrection of the dead?" To meet this doubt he brings together, in a summary statement, the whole evidence of the Gospel. The direct proof of Christ's resurrection, witnessed by five hundred brethren at once, " of whom the greater part remain unto this present;" and then, after the most distinct enforcement of the inference, he comes to the natural apprehension of human doubt, and with wonderful skill touches upon the mystery that reason cannot dispel: " But some will say how are the dead raised up? and with what body do they come?" Now the Apostle does not (as might seem from a hasty glance) attempt to answer this vain question, but with infinite tact he strikes at the very source of the error it expresses. He does not, nor could he tell, or the questioner understand, in what way the scattered element of frail mortality might be recombined, or by what other process the spiritual essence be re-invested with corporeal members. But he rebukes the folly of the implication, that this result cannot happen because it is inconceivable to the doubter. "I do not tell you"—we may paraphrase the argument—"how you are to be re-embodied, but I tell you that the very process in which you think the difficulty to consist, is constantly occurring before your eyes"—" Thou fool, that which thou sowest is not quickened unless it die"—a reply derived from the analogy of nature. If we were not habitually familiar with this last common result, were it only a scientific inference or historic statement, the question of the Sadducee is just what would be heard. To look on that small grain, dry and hard, and seemingly deprived of that life which it possessed while yet hanging on the parent stem, it would be hard to believe that when cast into the dust of the earth, from it a new living frame of vegetation is to rise. No scrutiny can discover the germ of its future life; it is unlife-like matter; it might well be asked with what body shall *it* come? Yet see what follows; as the spring advances, at the moment appointed by the Creator alike for man and nature, the living plant has risen, and spreads its bright head to the sun of a new season of life; how unlike the seed that has just died—the body that was committed to the dust; from whence, one might ask, that tall stem, that broad green leaf, that bright consummate flower—can this be that body? But the Apostle answers, "And that thou sowest, thou sowest not that body that shall be. . . . . but God giveth it a body as it hath pleased Him, to every seed his own body." The seed contains in itself some germ of life, manifestly framed to endure after its death, and capable of new development, by some unknown assimilation, contrived by the Giver of Life. Though the vegetable process must be very different from that to which the Apostle compares it, it yet no less answers the doubt. In the human frame there is a *sensible* germ of life, to be known by those properties already described as wholly distinct from any properties known to be material; thoughts, sentiments, powers of far-reaching communion, —to grasp the past and future, and to embody the non-existent—the germ of a being not conceivably within any known processes of dissolution—a self-consciousness distinct from all bodily sense—to outlive the body's death, and be clothed upon with that new and glorious frame which the Apostle describes as the spiritual body: this we may presume to be the indestructible germ of future life. Such, indeed, is a notion which has always forced itself on reflection—the thinking mind's anticipation for itself —but still offering itself rather as an aspiration than as a conviction. The most profound of ancient philosophers, who attempted to prove the soul's immortality, felt the want of a revelation, and concluded justly that it must be looked for.

All things earthly are, it is known, compounded out of a few elementary substances, of which not one ceases to be. The chemist can follow, by weight or volume, the transition of each elementary atom. And all known substances are but known proportions into which these subtle and effective, though separately invisible, elements combine. One *element alone obeys not, nor appears;* the most powerful agent at the command of science can disclose no element of all-commanding and all-moving mind. Universally operative as the sole source of order in modes having no material analogy—it is wholly and uniformly an untraceable existence; in vain the chemist, or the anatomist, or the physiologist may look for the living among the dead: the living, deathless particle has escaped from its envelopements of earth and gaseous matter, to be again at once, or at the allotted time, " clothed upon ;" to receive again from its Creator a body, " as it hath pleased Him."

The doubt here intended to be met is the aptest to come, and hardest to shake off. Such is the natural infirmity of reason. In this, our transitory and clouded state, the dark side of the future is turned to human sense, if unenlightened by spiritual convictions, and the visual beam of faith. Man can conceive but one state of life, and this he sees ever passing, he knows not whither; the sepulchral image of mortality stands dark and stern before him; graves, and worms, and epitaphs, the coffin, and the shroud terminate his view. The sad question forces itself not on his reason, but on his fancy. He cannot help asking that vain question asked by the heathen philosopher, and by the unbelieving Sadducee, and repeated, with as little wisdom, by the moral poet, who asks—

"When shall spring visit the mouldering urn?"

That same lifeless dust from which man's mortal frame was borrowed for a season, and which, by a just sentence, claims back the loan—" for dust thou art and unto dust shalt thou return,"—is itself but material in the hand of Omnipotence; the rich wardrobe of ten hundred million of attires ; of living frames and silent growing flowers ; and, at the same Will, can reproduce the body as it reproduces the flower. He who has clothed the lily " that Solomon in all his glory was not equal to one of these," can waken up from the dust of the grave, a more glorious form, never more to enter there.

How this event must come to pass it is but folly to inquire. It must be ; it is the promise of Him who is to perform it. Man is handed into life, unconscious and helpless. With as little aid from self, with as little apprehensions of the manner, he will rise in the presence, and by the will of a higher power. This is declared to him as " a mystery," but *proved* as a certain fact. He knows that this year's corn will rise, only because the corn of former years has risen. He has precisely the same warrant for himself, for " now is Christ risen from the dead, and become the first-fruits of them that slept ; for since by man came death, by man also came resurrection of the dead." Can proof go further? a natural presumption ; a Divine promise ; a clear instance.

It is one among the many distinguishing marks of a wisdom superior to human philosophy, that a question on which every class and school, ancient and modern, has wasted all the resources of ingenuity, only to illustrate its unattainable nature—is thus disposed of with a simple precision that sets it at once in its just light—clearly indicating the difficulty, and stopping at the necessary limit. To illustrate this distinction would ask a voluminous though little instructive history of what all the most eminent sects of heathen and scholastic philosophy have done to solve this great mystery of nature. The mind of all ages, from "thrice great Hermes" to Leibnitz or Des Cartes, has worked vainly at this one problem; but still so as to add a clear and forcible indication to those already mentioned, of that "longing after immortality"—that instructive sense of its own nature, which has been implanted by Him who has made the soul to live, and confirmed it by the Word of life and the great example of the Resurrection.

NOTE D.

EVIDENCE.

I have mentioned, among the essential adaptations to be antecedently sought, in a religion of Divine institution, that of direct accrediting indications of its origin and authority, such as being seen or admitted should leave no doubt as to their nature. Without this, the strongest presumption, from any amount of wisdom or moral excellence, would be insufficient for the purpose of public institution, or to satisfy the demands of a faith in objects not in any way presentable to sense, nor sustained by any social influences. There is no rule of human judgment so precise as to fix an exact limit to the measure of man's attainments in moral theory; nor are the average measure of intellect, or the ordinary rules of reason and experience adequate to the laborious analysis, or the breadth of survey, that may discern both in the doctrines and history of religion, the chain of prescience, or the amount of designing wisdom inconsistent with any human origin.

If then such direct and sensible proof be thus essentially requisite, how is it to be explained that among the Christian multitude so comparatively few are apparently acquainted with the express proofs and testimonies of the creed they hold? I will not, in answering this question, touch on the sad infusion of the evil spirit of unbelief which prevails in the religion of the world : this is no result of any want of proof. But the fact is, that the object of the great body of testimony on which the Gospel holds its ground (under Providence) among the firmest institutions of the civilized world, is in some degree misconceived. It is the great muniment of church and state acceptance, fixed and established in the body of all authorized sanctions; of the wisdom, learning, and immemorial consent of the best minds of ages. It is fully known to exist, and to have ever resisted the hostility of its enemies, but it is not and was not designed to be the foundation of faith to individuals.

Are we, then, left to the mercy of the sceptic's common taunt, that the Gospel is received without any ground in reason by the Christian. The contrary is the fact. The *New Testament* contains *in itself* the very clearest evidence : sense conveys no stronger, and men misjudge the testimony of sense. When once received on the common ground of universal admission, it offers a very strong and impressive appeal to the reason of every reader, who gives that ordinary attention which is usually bestowed on any earnest perusal by a sincere mind. All the main conditions which go to establish Paley's conclusion are then clearly and unmistakeably presented, not in the shape of an argument, of all forms the least effectual upon the faith of men, but so as to convey the ordinary impression inseparable from plain fact, on the judgment and common sense. There is thus a latent argument which impresses the reason according to its customary habits, and carries an implicit conviction to the sincere mind. Something depends on the attention, but this is equally true in all cases. No argument can be more simply clear in its premises or unanswerable in its conclusions, than that which implicitly conveys itself to the scripture student's conception. The conclusion is suppressed; it no more requires distinct statement than the plainest consequence of any common practical proceeding; and, if needful, could with logical accuracy be maintained from facts within the compass of the believer's faith. Let me briefly follow out this process. I have already stated the general ground on which the New Testament is received. Receiving the Gospel narrative on this common ground, the serious reader finds its proofs in all its statements, whether of word or deed, the character, acts, precepts, and manifest motives of all the actors. These indications, in no degree inferior to the evidence of sense, carry all their intrinsic force of conviction, without any logical process further than must tacitly or latently belong to every habitual impression. This impression (setting aside for the present the witness of the spirit) can be stated in the form of an argument of which each step can be proved in detail, beyond the reach of any answer. The witnesses of the New Testament could not have been deceived, they could not have deceived others: these two inferences follow from the nature of the facts: and lastly, that *if possible*, they would not have committed any deception, equally follows from the precepts and moral systems they taught, and from the fact that there was an utter absence of motives. I do not go further into the numerous corroborative circumstances, as I only desire to shew that self-evidence which no sincere mind can miss—an evidence full enough for the purpose of God.

But there is a strong distinction between the impression of truth inevitably communicated to all who look sincerely to the source and the credentials, upon the authority of which a system or a creed is handed down and accepted by the world. The world admits Christianity as a fact established on incontrovertible grounds of authority and unshaken testimony, which has been open to the criticism of more than eighteen centuries, and assailed in vain by all the resources of human hostility. This, too, is universally understood, and holds its place among popular impressions, insomuch that numbers give their assent who are not yet otherwise to be ranked as believers in any true sense. Thus, though we should admit the often repeated reproach of the unbeliever, that the multitude have no actual proof for their belief, still it is to be answered that we do not offer popular assent as any part of our evidence. It cannot be objected truly that the Christian community holds its creed on grounds similar to the Mahometan, or Brahmin, or any barbaric superstition. The religion of civilization, which has passed the scrutiny of eighteen centuries of literary and scientific progress, which has, for many centuries of the highest intellectual culture, been exposed to the free hostility of the most searching scepticism, upon which all the resources of the most extensive learning, criticism, and logical talent of ages have been lavished, the evidences of which have challenged reply without having elicited any, satisfactory even to the common sense of an unbeliever—such a creed must at least be admitted to stand on ground wholly peculiar to itself. Under such conditions, it may fairly be said that it is received because it is established on irrefragable testimony, just as the facts of science and the principles of commerce are understood by the few and received by the many. All this is, perhaps, too obvious, but it is worthy of special notice, because the common class of unbelievers, as ignorant as those whom they address, deal in strong appeals to ignorance: that there is no proof of Christianity; that it exists by popular credulity alone, or as a result of education; but that it is to be inferred from the entire conduct of professing Christians, that this belief is not genuine; that if questioned, nobody can state the reason of his faith. Now it is not unimportant that it should be understood that such ignorance is no test of insincerity, and does not amount to any objection: and, therefore, that if it be alleged as proof of the insincerity of popular faith, the objection is a fallacy. It is quite true, from wholly different causes, fully stated in the foregoing argument, and accounted for in Scripture itself, that in the religion of the multitude there is a large infusion of unbelief. Of this it may be observed that it by no means rests on denials, objections, or want of proof. On the contrary, it is in many instances combined with *fullest assent on grounds of proof*, and in most without denial. But in the not few cases in which faith is quite sincere, there are, besides the latent proof already mentioned, other influences of still more force than any proof can have. The spiritual power of the Gospel is soon felt; the moral system offering its evidence, and working its effects by Divine aid, carry with them their own proof and all the living influences which distinguish reality from illusion. It never was designed that a faith given to alter the most rooted corruptions of man's nature was to be the simple result of an argument. The actual uses of proof are overlooked by the sceptic; it never was designed for the purposes he assumes; no arguments can

"Administer to a mind diseased,"

or change the moral nature. But without tangible credentials suited to the reason, and conformable to the rule of all instituted law in civilized nations, no creed could be adopted in accordance with those principles on which all social institutions stand secure. Every age, perhaps every generation, brings forth its popular delusions and superstitious impostures, that carry away crowds ready to worship error on the impulse by which they might follow truth : but the stamp of critical sanction is withheld; the authenticating credential of a Divine authority is wanting, and they are swept away in the stream of which men's sin and error are the froth and bubbles.

As I have said, the Gospels and other apostolic writings carry not mere precept and doctrine. They are, in fact, clear statements of the whole substance of the proof; they even present the whole inference; the argument consists of a full, explicit statement of unquestionable acts of Divine power; of reasons for its exertion; of intended consequences. No sincere student of Scripture can fail to become sensible to this. All that remains for reason to do is to ascertain that those writings are the genuine productions of the witnesses. This the historical critic proves, the pious believer admits. He is aware of the full consent of historic record, and the concurrence of opinion on a matter in which its general competence is admitted; but the *virtual* argument is *an actual part* of his faith.

There is one consideration which has often forced itself upon me, in respect of the subject of evidence. There is a tendency very often to be observed among Christians, which cannot but be hurtful to faith. I mean the espousal of some special branch of doctrine, on which their respective modes of opinion and conversation seem to be absorbed and spent. I have frequently listened to very zealous Christians, whose whole conversation turned on the earnest, and sometimes angry, enforcement of the doctrine of decrees, to the entire exclusion of any other view: others I have heard with equal exclusiveness dwell on the contrary doctrine: some on the prophetic view of the latter times, or the second advent; and, in like manner, on each of every possible view of Scripture or theology. Now I do not, of course, object to the discussion of any doctrinal opinion, but my observation is, that a special and partial adoption of a favorite doctrine tends gradually to expand itself into the place of religion, and thus, if it should not in some measure exclude, at least it must tend to sap and weaken the influence of faith.

I have further had occasion to notice a very important

affection, of a somewhat similar tendency, common to those who have to strive against the natural unbelief of their own nature. Their mistake is the same which I have already adverted to in this note, of expecting to find an effectual remedy in argumentative proofs. Many and forceable as these are, such is not their intent: man is not subject to moral convictions from mere reason.

Now, taking these two last-mentioned popular errors together, they have the common effect of turning the mind from the proper and prescribed object of faith—the Saviour.

But what I would urge is, a constant and close retention of the great crowning evidence of the Resurrection—a fact offered on the most accessible testimony, and carrying in itself the clearest assurance where assurance is most wanting. It is in this aspect it is offered by St. Paul, 1 Cor. xv., and it thus combines the shortest and most definite proof, specially directed to, and connected with, the main end and immediate object of the Christian's faith. It is in the wholly unmistakeable event of the Resurrection, proved by " many infallible proofs," that the Great Apostle proclaims the assurance of the Christian's hope. Here is the glorious reality, directly casting a sure light into the valley of death; upon the dark barrier from which no other light returns; round which the natural terrors of mortality hang in dread suspense and awe; in the gloomy signlessness of which involuntary doubts arise, and the fearful question, " With what body do they come?" The triumphant answer is given, to carry peace and rest to mortal fear,—" But now is Christ risen from the dead, and become the first-fruits of them that slept." Here is a matter of fact, that has in it no mystery and no room for doubt. All the arguments that ever were written contain no stronger certainty, in a few words, as plain and clear for the dullest and most unlettered apprehension as for the most acute or learned—1 Cor., xv., 4-8 ; and again, Acts 1, 3-10. In this event the Gospel takes a sensible form, and collects itself into an intelligible fact, which rejects all subtle questions and discouraging doubts ; "As in Adam all die, so in Christ shall all be made alive," a promise confirmed by a visible fact, on which Christian faith and hope can rest serene and confident amid the lapse of passing things and paths tracked by footsteps leading to the grave.

It is, I am convinced, a wise provision of the Creator for the conduct of this world's course, that the reasoning faculty is not very highly developed in the mass of mankind, and that the motives by which we mostly are governed and guided are the ordinary result of experience, and the discipline of habit. But for this we should be making such mistakes in the commonest concerns, as are committed in those aspiring speculations which are flattered with the name of philosophy. And it is happily so ordered, in adaptation to the ordinary constitution of the intellect and moral nature, that faith, supported by a strong reserve of irrefragable evidence, is far more practically realized by training, moral experience, and that spiritual influence which " gives the increase." But one fact may be taken as a rule and a test ; to be true and effective it must be the *habit* of the mind. *Man cannot be anything truly that he is not habitually.* Though one should rise from the dead to warn or convince, the impression would pass if not constantly entertained. It would be as the seed sown on the stony ground, and having no roots. Hence the watchfulness, the "prayer without ceasing," the denial of worldly distractions, the affections set "on things above," and all the similar exhortations of the Apostles and their Master.

NOTE E.

THE TEMPTATION.

THERE is no incident in the entire Scripture narrative that seems to have challenged more dissent from the sceptic mind, than the narrative of the first sin and its consequences. And one consequence has been a very inconsiderate attempt to explain that narrative into some figurative sense. I shall not here stop to discuss how far such constructions may be founded on any just principle. For, in whatever manner that narrative is considered, it is most striking, (on any patient contemplation of the history of man, and that of the religion of Scripture,) to discern the manner in which that account falls in with and forms a consistent part of the whole. Like every other part of that history, it wants all the usual characters of human invention. For an invention, it is told with a simplicity and want of imaginative circumstance: a mythological inventor, or a compiler of oriental traditions, would have conceived or found some enormity more apparently proportioned to the importance of the event and the actors; and if we look to its essential connexion with the whole of a succession of dispensations, occupying nearly twenty-four centuries, from Noah to Christ, it must be seen that in its main substance the temptation of the first parents is what should be looked for.

It has been objected to on the ground of Divine justice : the lightness of the offence and the severity of the sentence. I have, as fully as such objections can require, already considered these questions, and shewn that the offence was not light or the punishment unduly severe.*

In whatever degree the language of Genesis may be considered as mystical, the fact must yet be substantively as represented. It is implied in all that follows: it offers the key to every part of the whole of the Scripture writings, and also the only just explanation of profane history and the state of man. The narrative of Genesis is the appropriate prologue to the great drama of man.

But it derives no small confirmation from another incident not dissimilar in its purport, occupying a like place in the commencement of the great remedial dispensation, and not without a direct relation to that first event in Eden : " As in Adam all die, even so in Christ shall all be made alive." The temptation in the wilderness followed on the temptation in the garden :—he who was to "fulfil all righteousness,"—to conquer where man fell— was to meet the adversary of man, as man. A seed of

---

* Vestiges of God in Scripture, p. 47.

the woman, who should bruise the old serpent's head, was to be born; and the time, fixed by a long line of prophecy, could not fail to be known to the enemy thus deeply concerned. To meet that second man as he had met the first was the obvious course of the same adversary. It is in the highest degree probable that, during the forty days assigned to this great controversy, temptations more proportioned to the several characters so engaged in spiritual conflict may have been used; these were not within the powers of language or human comprehension and were unnecessary to record. In the communication of the event, our Lord manifestly had respect to his never-ceasing purpose of example to his followers; and what is remarkable is, that the narrative has manifest respect to those forms of temptation to which man in his present state is exposed, and offers at the same time the proper instruction for resistance. Against the casuistry which pleads in defence of sinful influences—sensuality, pride, ambition, and worldliness—there is a direct appeal to the letter and the testimony—" it is written."

NOTE F.

ON THE UNIVERSE.

THE argument by which I have met the objections stated in Lecture VI. derives its entire value from the fact that it proceeds on the sceptic's own grounds. It follows him into an *extension* of the analogy of present and known existence, to an unknown state, and shows that upon his own assumptions his conclusions are untrue.

To pretend, however, that any certain inference respecting the universal constitution of the Divine government, or the antecedent policy of the disclosures of Revealed Religion, can be derived from any argument, would be but to repeat the very error of the objection. Christianity, viewed in its whole comprehension, manifestly originates from an antecedent state of things, wholly past the reach of human philosophy. The assumptions of the sceptic or the no less daring theologian are equally presumptuous and unwarranted.

There are nevertheless in the conditional solution upon which I have ventured, some grounds of assumption which I do not consider it equally necessary to abandon. There can be no reasonable doubt as to the sensible evidence of the vast and inconceivable extent of the universe. And the grounds in reason are fully sufficient for the affirmation of a universal prevalence of life and moral order. Here I think rational inference stops: we have, it is true, some glimpses of Divine light, on the authority of Scripture; but they offer nothing to the grasp of reasonable speculation. That there exists a vast population of angels—of souls—that there are evil beings and a spiritual enemy—that there is a spiritual government extending to all existence: so far we can ascertain on grounds of authority, confirmed by facts and probability. Beyond this, all speculation must be doubtful. So far, it may be of some importance as tending to repress human presumption, and to check the questions which are ever starting up out of the obscurity and narrowness of human reason—that there should be established some clear general conception of what can be certainly affirmed. Man overrates himself and the little space of creation he holds: it were well if he could be taught to look from the Psalmist's point of view, " For I will consider the heavens which are the work of thy fingers, and the moon and stars which thou hast ordained. What is man that thou art mindful of him, and the son of man that thou visitest him?"* That this feeling was entertained as a devotional element in the Psalmist's mind, is expressed by many beautiful and sublime allusions, in which he refers to the magnificence and vastness of God's creation, in contrast with the littleness and the transitory duration of man.

And yet when the sacred poet so vividly felt and expressed that mighty truth, and appealed so solemnly to the field of creation, he was far indeed from any adequate conception of that stupendous attestation of Divine power and glory. It was then, as indeed it still must ever be to earthly sense, far beyond the most expansive conception. But the science of modern time has widely thrown back the bounds of the known creation, and put man in possession of realities large beyond imagination. We can measure with instrumental precision, and express with the accuracy of numbers, bulks and distances beyond the scope of vision; and still find ourselves but at the foot of the illimitable height. Distances expressed

* Psalm VIII. According to Calmet the author of this Psalm is unknown.

by millions of millions of miles are revealed but as units in the vaster measure of still further distances. Motions equally inconceivable in their velocity are reduced, in those vast distances, to the seeming of stillness; and yet no sign of an end. When science has spent its whole resource, it only finds the starred infinite before it still. Light, travelling 192,000 miles per second, travels on upon its eternal way, fulfilling its functions, conveying its intelligence to eyes and souls, telling the goodness and proclaiming the glory of God to the people of unnumbered provinces of the infinite empire of the Creator. In that illimitable dominion a depth of distance might be taken, compared with which our solar system, nearly 6,000,000,000* statute miles across, would be reduced to a viewless point, while the aspect of the starry sphere would appear undiminished in brightness. In the eternal course of providential rule, a time may be assigned compared with which earth's history from beginning to end must be an instant. How justly might the Psalmist say of man " a thing of nought, his time passeth away like a shadow." Through all this boundless realm there are the indications of one design, of living existence, of a Mind that organized, that upholds, and rules the whole; that is nowhere absent. The most invisible insect that creeps its laborious journey across its leaf, might as well be supposed to speculate on the laws of nations and the ways of men, as the profoundest philosophy approach the policy of that rule or the measure of that Mind.

* More nearly 5,782,668,205.

From this more enlarged aspect of Being the conclusion should be, that (however consistently a single chain of principle may pervade all,) still too minute a scope of that Whole meets our observation for the purpose of reasoning on the divine nature, or the divine plan, further than the explicit declarations of revealed religion. The analogy supplied by nature, and by the courses of providence and the moral order of life, carry us a little way : they do not confirm the sceptic's view; but, as Bishop Butler amply proves, so far as they can be applied, confirm the doctrines of Scripture. Those doctrines carry us a little way further up the line of the great argument : but it ascends past contemplation to a height shrouded with impenetrable mists—concealed by innumerable unknown possibilities.

But the sceptic has various moods ; and the same objections are made to follow from a depreciation of man. Not content with questioning the wisdom, justice, and love of the main doctrine of the cross, he asks contemptuously, for what ? The reply to this question is implicitly contained in the same answer already stated (Lect. VI.) ; but as the preceding observations may be taken in some respects as favoring the same disparaging views of man, I will add a few concluding remarks which appear to me as having some practical tendency. If this life were all—the importance of man would be small indeed, and the moral order of life of little more importance in the sum of things than the order of the jungle and the den. It might, indeed, be asked, not only, why we should assume all those vast arrangements to be made for man—but, indeed, why such a creature was made at all.

One sentence scatters these doubts and mistakes into thin air—man is immortal—the known object of a mighty system of divine arrangements—a soul—a spirit of essential life, to be developed into further new and glorious being; and of infinitely more importance in the divine plan, than all the countless masses of material frame that stand or roll through illimitable space. Man *is mind*, and so far in the image of his Creator. This globe of earth was made for him—its dominion expressly given to him—he is endowed with a heart to love his God—an understanding to study His works—a soul to look for future life. These were not meant for nothing.

From the first day of his creation to the present he has been the subject of divine laws and revelations. He alone pronounces the name of God on this earth; he has learnt to pray; he is taught to worship; whatever he *is*, he was designed for a high and holy end—God made him for Himself: through him the rebel Power assailed God's supremacy : for him the Prince of darkness watches : not unsuitably may the Son of God have taken flesh to atone for his sins—to expiate his dreadful lapse. If, as the sceptic objects, the disproportion between man and the visible system of things is too vast for the importance thus assigned, still, to the omnipotent God matter and motion and form and arrangement and time and space cost nothing : a grain of dust from a royal demesne were more. Far different is the case of spirit created by Him—to serve, to love, to witness,—to grow in goodness and wisdom, with an endless growth—to be happy with a boundless felicity in the presence of Him who "is love," and who delights in the happiness of those who love Him. Surely, even for one soul redeemed—snatched from the jaws of the worm "that shall not die"—fifty worlds like this, elaborated through an eternity of ages, appears as little. But consider the generations of six thousand years; consider this little globe as the womb of time, in which a world of eternity is maturing, and how easily the whole of these arrangements of which we speak fall into proportion and order.

But there is one serious reflection, How we are individually concerned?

If such were the preparations—such the comprehensive purpose, the steady and deliberate plan, in which we are thus an essential part and inextricably involved, what must it be to be found unworthy? In the orderly march of God's unerring purpose, are you a rebellious atom—striving so far as in you lies to frustrate that purpose— to nullify that creation—to defeat that redemption—to secure that victory to Satan? And, if so, will you presume to call in question the awful justice that dooms you to the last consequences of your own folly?

But there are more consolatory reflections. He who has done so much is our guardian and protector. He is on our side. To say he has made world upon world for us is but little: He has prepared for us a place in the higher realms of eternity—a realm of peace, and love, and joy, irradiated by the light of the presence of his own all-commanding majesty—in the companionship of angels, in the communion of saints—in the contemplation of his love and goodness and power, and of the boundless universe he has created—in high and holy light above the low realms of care and grief and bereavements—of pain and every form of woe.

THE END.

www.ingramcontent.com/pod-product-compliance
Lightning Source LLC
Chambersburg PA
CBHW021810230426
43669CB00008B/704